PATRIC

# ALTERNATIVE FEES FOR
# LITIGATORS
## AND THEIR CLIENTS

ABALAW
PRACTICE
DIVISION
The Business of Practicing Law

**Commitment to Quality:** The Law Practice Division is committed to quality in our publications. Our authors are experienced practitioners in their fields. Prior to publication, the contents of all our books are rigorously reviewed by experts to ensure the highest quality product and presentation. Because we are committed to serving our readers' needs, we welcome your feedback on how we can improve future editions of this book.

Cover design by RIPE Creative, Inc.

Nothing contained in this book is to be considered as the rendering of legal advice for specific cases, and readers are responsible for obtaining such advice from their own legal counsel. This book and any forms and agreements herein are intended for educational and informational purposes only.

The products and services mentioned in this publication are under trademark or service-mark protection. Product and service names and terms are used throughout only in an editorial fashion, to the benefit of the product manufacturer or service provider, with no intention of infringement. Use of a product or service name or term in this publication should not be regarded as affecting the validity of any trademark or service mark.

The Law Practice Division of the American Bar Association offers an educational program for lawyers in practice. Books and other materials are published in furtherance of that program. Authors and editors of publications may express their own legal interpretations and opinions, which are not necessarily those of either the American Bar Association or the Law Practice Division unless adopted pursuant to the bylaws of the Association. The opinions expressed do not reflect in any way a position of the Division or the American Bar Association, nor do the positions of the Division or the American Bar Association necessarily reflect the opinions of the author.

Printed in the United States of America.

**Library of Congress Cataloging-in-Publication Data**

Lamb, Patrick J. author.
 Alternative fees for litigators and their clients / Patrick Lamb.
  p. cm.
 Includes bibliographical references and index.
 ISBN 978-1-62722-332-4 (alk. paper)
 1. Lawyers--Fees--United States.  I. Title.
 KF316.L36 2014
 340.068'8--dc23

                                                          2014018716

Discounts are available for books ordered in bulk. Special consideration is given to state bars, CLE programs, and other bar-related organizations. Inquire at Book Publishing, American Bar Association, 321 North Clark Street, Chicago, Illinois 60654-7598.

www.ShopABA.org

# Contents

Lawyers Concerned for Lawyers, Inc.
31 Milk Street
Suite 810
Boston, MA 02109

*About the Author* ............................................................... *vii*

*Acknowledgments* ............................................................. *ix*

*Introduction* ..................................................................... *xi*

**Chapter 1**   The Status Quo Is Broken                                1

**Chapter 2**   Did the Great Reset Change Things?                      11

**Chapter 3**   Understanding the Terminology                           17

Structures That Are Not Alternative Fee Arrangements ............... 18

Structures That Are Alternative Fee Arrangements .................... 20

**Chapter 4**   What Works When?                                        27

**Chapter 5**   So Where Are We Now?                                    33

**Chapter 6**   Issues Created by AFAs                                  39

"We would have made more if we billed hourly." ...................... 39

"Please send me shadow bills." ........................................... 44

"What does a value fee engagement letter look like?" ................. 47

**Chapter 7**   The Tools That Make AFAs Work   **53**

**Chapter 8**   Early Case Assessment   **57**

**Chapter 9**   Process Mapping, Project Management, and Checklists   **63**

**Chapter 10**   Decision Trees   **77**

**Chapter 11**   Toward an Understanding of Risk and Spend   **83**

**Chapter 12**   Disaggregation   **85**

**Chapter 13**   After-Action Assessments   **93**

**Chapter 14**   The Client Experience   **99**

**Chapter 15**   Some Thoughts on Pricing   **107**
Time to Knowledge—Role in Pricing..................................... 111
Things That Always Seem to Come Up................................. 118

**Chapter 16**   Accounting Issues   **123**

**Chapter 17**   Ethical Considerations   **127**
Ethical Considerations in Structuring Value-Based Fees.............. 128
Value-Based Fees and the Philosophy of the ABA Model Rules ...... 131
Ensuring Reasonable Fees ................................................. 133
Performance-Based Fees in the Civil Context .......................... 136
Ethical Considerations in the Earning of a Flat Fee.................... 138

**Chapter 18**   Clients: Be Better Buyers   **141**

**Chapter 19**   The 50 Percent Challenge   **147**

**Chapter 20**   Making Change Happen                                    **155**

**Appendix**                                                                   **163**

After-Action Assessment Sample ........................................ 164
Checklist Sample. ....................................................... 165
Early Case Assessment .................................................. 170
Engagement Letter Sample ............................................. 176
Pricing Checklist. ....................................................... 179

**Index**                                                                     **181**

# About the Author

I am a litigator of some 30 years' experience. In the 1990s, I had the good fortune to represent a client who explained (in no uncertain terms) that my firm's failure to meet its budget had caused his company to miss its earnings estimates, with a resulting decrease in the price of the stock and, importantly, his personal net worth. His assertions may well have been apocryphal, but I liked representing him, so I took him seriously and learned to create budgets with teeth. My experience with him helped me move ahead on the pricing curve.

Since January 2008, I have been a partner of Valorem Law Group, a firm three colleagues and I founded. Our business model was and remains use of nonhourly fee arrangements to represent clients in complex commercial disputes. The firm has grown, and we've now applied the same pricing philosophy in patent litigation.

Since becoming an "alternative fee lawyer" in 2008, I can't tell you the number of times lawyers have told me they calculate a price for an alternative fee arrangement (AFA) by figuring out how many hours they will spend on a matter, multiplying that number by expected hourly rates, and using the sum as the proposed fee.

Sometimes they get "creative" and apply the firm's realization rate to the number to create a somewhat lower total.

Because many clients believe hourly rate fees are too high to begin with, this "wolf in sheep's clothing" pricing system merely replicates that which clients reject. Renaming hourly fees as alternative fees has robbed AFAs of their promise for clients. I want to explore why this happened and what options exist for those who sincerely want to use AFAs to create a better world for their clients (and their firms). My partners and I remain true believers that the benefits of properly priced alternative fees can enhance relationships between lawyers and clients. There is no Google map to get there, but I hope this book makes the journey a bit easier.

More about me and Valorem Law Group, which is so committed to providing value to its clients that every bill includes a Value Adjustment Line (allowing clients to rewrite the amount due to reflect the value the clients believe they received), can be found at www.valoremlaw.com.

# Acknowledgments

I would like to thank Nicole Auerbach and Mark Sayre, my part-ners, who have been with me since we began our journey in January 2008. We chose the name Valorem for our firm because we wanted to create value-driven relationships with our clients and believed our name should state our prime value. I have learned much from Nicole and Mark, and they have inspired me in ways I could not have imagined in 2008. I would also like to thank Dave Bohrer, who joined Valorem in 2013 and in our short time as partners has proven himself an able educator. And special thanks to Henry Turner Jr. for his assistance at several points along the road to publication.

Valorem is one of the few firms that has an advisory board, and I would like to thank our board for their input in this project. I am indebted to Jeff Carr, general counsel of FMC Technologies and the leading voice for value-based billing; Paul Lippe, CEO of Legal OnRamp; David Graham of DSW (best shoes ever); and Gerry Riskin, the founder of the global powerhouse legal consultancy Edge International. All have advised me on countless occasions and freely shared their wisdom and insight.

I also would like to thank Ray Bayley and Lois Haubold, princi-pals of Novus Law, and Lisa Damon of Seyfarth Shaw for teaching me about the value of process engineering and the real value it can generate for clients.

Finally, I would like to thank Tom Mighell, former chair of the ABA Law Practice Management Section, for generously helping me navigate the pathway toward publishing this book. His insights and encouragement were always appreciated.

To the extent there are good ideas in this book, they are the product of the insights of my partners and these advisors. To the extent the ideas are not up to standard, it is because I did not collaborate enough with these extraordinary people.

# Introduction

*"I think we are seeing in many ways that value-based billing alone is not going to carry the day. If the law firm provides services the exact same way it did under a billable hour arrangement, nothing has changed. There is no risk sharing."*
—Ken Grady, former general counsel, Wolverine Worldwide Inc.

September 15, 2008. That is the date Lehman Brothers filed for bankruptcy. It also is the date many observers claim marked a turning point for the legal profession, ushering in a period of extraordinary upheaval for corporate clients, law firms, and, most recently, law schools. Others claim the Lehman Brothers collapse and related economic meltdown merely accelerated preexisting conditions. Does it matter who's right? Not really, other than perhaps to provide historical clarity. The point is that the profession is in a time of unprecedented change. Law departments have been forced to do more with fewer resources. They, in turn, have made the same demand on their law firms. Law firms have been forced to slash expenses and head count to satisfy their partners' demands for profits. Law school graduates have been unable to find jobs. And so on. We all read about it. We all feel it. We all know it. Some have taken advantage of the changing conditions. Others seem to be hoping to wake up in a cold sweat having just experienced a nightmare.

One key part of the change has been in the area of fees. Fairly or not, alternative fee arrangements, or AFAs, are at the center of the discussions about change, or at least close to it. Despite the great promise of nonhourly fees, their potential is not being realized, and both clients and lawyers are becoming disenchanted. Many law firm lawyers are hoping this disenchantment leads to a return to the good old days when hours were billed, rates increased every year more than inflation, realization rates were high, and client complaints few. (Somewhere, the casts of *Happy Days* and *Leave It to Beaver* are laughing about how the good old days only existed on television screens.)

Apart from the fantasies of some, those times are long gone. To be certain, clients know they are gone forever. Just ask any general counsel if it would be a good career move to request that the CEO return to growing the law department budget by 10 percent or more every year. Clients know the reality is precisely the opposite of the fantasy: every year, they have to do more with less. Much more. Clients are searching for something that will help them meet this challenge because they know they will continue to confront it for the foreseeable future.

Some outside lawyers also know the old days are not returning. Others delude themselves into believing things will get better, and still others just hunker down in their foxholes and hope they get to retirement before anything drastic happens.

The issue, however, is not just the price or the type of fee structure. The hidden, less focused-upon issue is the cost of providing the services clients need. For many lawyers, AFAs were seen as the panacea, the solution to virtually all problems associated with the out-of-control system in place when the economy crashed and lawyers and clients were confronted with a stark new requirement to provide more at a lower price. But alternative fee arrangements are simply one of many tools that must be deployed to confront the "more with less" reality. Deploying AFAs without other tools is akin to trying to build a house with only a hammer—no saws, chisels, plastering tools, and so forth. A tool that lowers the price to clients but does not lower the cost of producing the work doesn't contribute to enhanced profitability. Most lawyers refused to focus on the cost of producing outcomes for their clients and complained that AFAs simply were price discounts.

Many, if not most, law firms refused to embrace the multi-tool approach. It was hard enough to adapt to the alternative fee world, though firms soon discovered that speaking the alternative fee language was simple. Many firms proclaimed they were offering alternative fees if they provided a discount to their hourly rates. Others realized that if they ginned up some large number and called it a fixed fee, they were offering alternative fees. But the greater challenge of altering business models, changing personnel planning and practices, eliminating the up-and-out model of advancement, partnering with outsourcing vendors, and taking so many other steps created a composite challenge that most firms have ignored.

On the flip side, clients know they cannot continue with the status quo. They know that change takes time, and if there is anything in short supply among in-house lawyers, it is time. As a result, they are willing to move to a better place if their natural skepticism can be overcome. But confronting natural skepticism and the paralysis it engenders is an equally formidable challenge.

My friend and mentor Jeffrey Carr, the general counsel of FMC Technologies, has a list of words that should be in the dictionary. He says that lawyers practice "complexification." That is, we take what we are doing and make it more complex, perhaps as a way of convincing people that it has greater importance. My own contribution to Carr's list is "processification," meaning lawyers' natural tendency to focus on process rather than outcome. Most of us have heard discussion of the difference between a litigator and a trial lawyer. The latter does what is needed to prepare to present the case to a jury and eschews other activity, while the former does whatever can be done. The point Carr drives home is that most lawyers are not focused on what is most important to their clients—outcomes. This creates an enormous and critical gap between lawyer and client.

Because actual change is too hard, outside lawyers co-opted the language of alternative fees. Clients know, however, that most of the alternative fees firms offer are anything but. They differ little from the highest hourly rate totals that would otherwise be budgeted to handle a matter, *and frequently the quoted alternative is higher.* This wolf-in-sheep's-clothing form of fee calculation is a surrogate to hourly billing, not a meaningful alternative to it. But firms dress hourly fees in the clothing of alternative fees and convince themselves they are offering clients something worthwhile. Clients see through this and understand that these are not alternative fees as they understand that term. They know these fees are not game changers that will help them do more with less. So clients see these surrogates as a cynical attempt to continue the status quo, allowing law firm partners to increase profits per partner and other metrics without helping the clients achieve the real change they need to accomplish. Is it any wonder clients are, by and large, unhappy with their firms?

In the midst of this unhappiness, however, is at least anecdotal evidence that clients and firms who have jointly embraced AFAs and the tools that make AFAs positive to the bottom lines of both client and firm are forging stronger, more positive relationships. The goals of this book are to identify some potential solutions that defy both the complexification and processification lawyers gravitate toward and to present some ideas that will help clients and their outside counsel achieve real results and unlock the potential of alternative fees.

Before moving on, I want to share a thought on how to get the most from this book. It is not an academic undertaking, and no effort has been made to comb the literature to find every story and example that might be useful. While that effort might have made this book much better, my day job (I'm a full-time trial lawyer) did not allow the time investment. Instead, I've used the lessons my colleagues and I have learned in our six-year experiment with a firm built on use of nonhourly billing arrangements. The result is that this book, for better or worse, is a collection of my insights, my thinking, and my opinions.

One of the ramifications of this is that my background, experience, and practice color everything I write. I write about my world, my experiences, my clients. I grew up in a big firm, spent seven years at a thirty-five-lawyer boutique (measured by Chicago standards), and then started Valorem with three friends in 2008. The firm has now grown to twelve. But at each place, I've represented the same clientele—Fortune 1000 companies and the businesses that do business with such companies. Some might think this is a book about "BigLaw," but it really is about people who represent the same types of clients as I do. Those clients influence the behavior of their lawyers, and this book at its core is about providing better service for those clients, regardless of the number of lawyers in a firm.

I believe there are lessons here to be gleaned for anyone with a litigation practice, representing individuals or corporations, in a small firm or a multinational behemoth, in a small town or a large city. But since I haven't walked a mile in the shoes of those whose practices are different from mine, I will try to make note of how these lessons might apply to other practices and hope you'll understand if I miss an insight or express an opinion that doesn't fit what you do and where you do it. That said, I know there is "idea fodder" in the pages that follow. Since this isn't a recipe book for everyone, you will have to consider the information I share in light of your own experiences, personality, and practice to see what changes are worth trying.

# Chapter 1
## THE STATUS QUO IS BROKEN

The system most of us grew up with is broken. Whether you are a client or an outside lawyer, the system is no longer working the way it used to. Instead of moving with our usual sure footing, we are "walking on ice with blindfolds on," where every move could cause us to slip and fall.

If you are a general counsel, or if you work for one, you may face the herculean effort of reducing your total legal spend by 30 percent. Or 40 percent. Or 20 percent. Whatever the percentage, the task is daunting. Even if you are only required to "stay flat," you face a tough challenge because the demands on each dollar are growing and firms continue to increase their rates.

Some have tried convergence programs, reducing the number of firms in the hope that concentrating work will lower fees. Some have tried discounts. Most run a tight ship. But when companies struggle in this sluggish economy, CEOs and CFOs clarify their expectations that legal departments do more with less—sometimes much less. At the same time, these companies are searching the globe for more and better opportunities. As a result, the amount of work most law departments must provide is increasing dramatically.

More compliance. More contracts. More litigation. More countries. More with less is the new normal for law departments.

Meanwhile, law firms have been dealing with unparalleled economic upheaval, growing churn with partners moving between firms, and unprecedented demand to simultaneously show high profits per partner. Law firm leaders have attacked these problems as they have so many others—by raising hourly rates. Mike Roster, former general counsel of Stanford and the chairman of the ACC Value Challenge, recently shared data illustrating the problem, shown in Figure 1.1:

**Figure 1.1**   Rising Costs

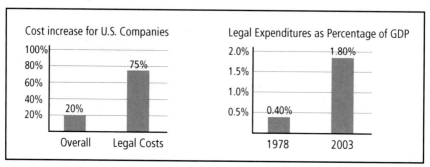

Confronted with this, the normal reaction by in-house lawyers has been to do one of two things. One is to try to extract more from the hourly rate piñata, and the other is to cut rates. For a few years, in-house lawyers were able to rely on the visual salve of firms cutting their rates, however reluctantly. That era is over. In October 2013, CounselLink reported that the average hourly rate paid (not charged) increased 2.7 percent year over year. In five of the leading markets, fees charged increased at a similar percentage and have done so over a longer time. In a recent three-year period, the compound annual growth rate was over 2.5 percent.[1] A report by the

---

1. One needs to keep the impact of reports like this in mind when looking forward, especially reports like the one from CounselLink, which is so data rich. With firms just starting the process for setting rates for 2014, the data will drive many to increase their rates or increase them more than they otherwise might.

Corporate Executive Board (CEB) and TyMetrix states that rates increased 7.3 percent from 2010 to 2012 (total inflation rate for same period was 5.96 percent). Many firms are again raising their rates faster than the rate of inflation.

Few expect clients to simply surrender, and they have not. A data set (see Figure 1.2) presented by Peer Monitor[2] shows rapidly declining realization rates (the percentage of the firm's total fees paid by the client) and the response to that phenomenon—continually increasing rates. Firms charge more, but clients respond by paying less of the amounts billed.

**Figure 1.2**   Realization Rates and Rate Progression

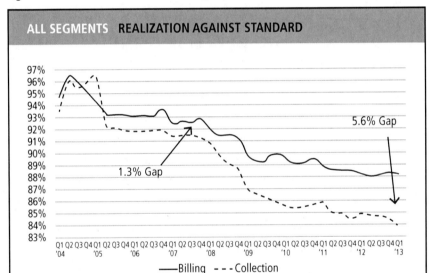

---

2. With permission. Peer Monitor, part of Thomson Reuters, is a benchmarking program that provides participating firms real-time economic data. Unlike many reports that are based on surveys and information shared selectively by firms, Peer Monitor's reports pull directly from participating firms' time and billing data.

**Figure 1.2** (continued)

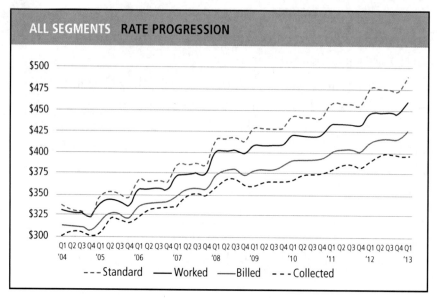

While clients are paying more, they are not paying more as fast as firms are billing more. The conclusion compelled by the data is that the financial relationship between law firms and their clients continues to be troublesome for both sides, and the trend is in favor of worsening problems. The data is not encouraging.

In the midst of this financial kerfuffle, client satisfaction with lawyers has plummeted.[3] While this dissatisfaction rarely translates into firing a law firm, it does translate into not hiring the offending firm for future matters. Dissatisfaction is also evidenced when clients move work in-house. In 2012, corporate counsel shifted $5.8 billion of work in-house.[4]

To paraphrase Herbert Stein's law: Trends that can't continue, won't. Clients can't meet the demand to do more with less when

---

3. BTI Consulting Group, "After 5-Year Upward March, Client Satisfaction Plummets," *The Mad Clientist* (blog), June 25, 2013, http://www.btibuzz.com/buzz/2013/6/25/after-5-year-upward-march-client-satisfaction-plummets.html.

4. BTI Consulting Group, "Corporate Counsel Shift $5.8 Billion In-House," *The Mad Clientist* (blog), June 20, 2013, http://www.btibuzz.com/buzz/2013/6/20/corporate-counsel-shift-58-billion-in-house.html.

their firms are demanding more. Firms, for their part, are facing massive economic stress because of the mobility of partners with large books of business and the growing demands to increase market share and show higher profits per partner. While it is impossible to accurately predict how the economic relationship between firms and clients will evolve, it is certain to play out at a faster pace than we have previously witnessed.

What options are typically considered? The traditional approaches are the economic ones—volume discounts, capped fees, blended rates, and similar efforts to limit hourly charges. The data does not support the hope that these efforts will reduce legal spend, as shown in Figure 1.3.

**Figure 1.3**   AFAs: Perceived Effectiveness vs. Actual Impact

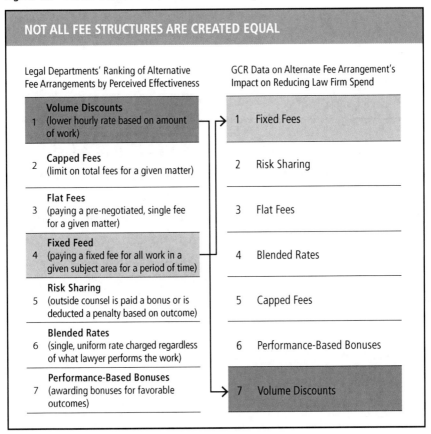

A different look (see Figure 1.4) at the same phenomenon is illuminating.

**Figure 1.4**  AFAs: Perceived Effectiveness at Cost Reduction[5]

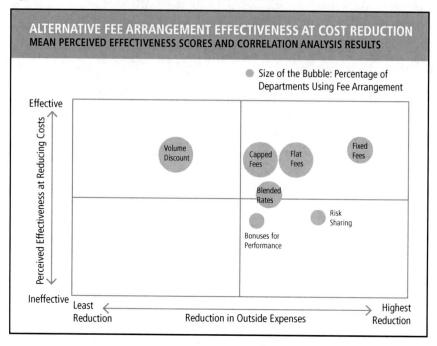

Why do the traditional options fail? More work done inefficiently does not lower per unit cost. Likewise, blended fees result in work being pushed to lower-priced lawyers, who frequently are more inefficient. But at its core, the flaw with the limited hourly rates approach is that it places the inside lawyer in a no-win position. Steven Greenspan, associate general counsel for litigation at United Technologies, in a recent presentation with Lisa Damon of Seyfarth Shaw, summarized the problems with hourly billing as shown in Figure 1.5.

---

5. Figures 1.3 and 1.4 courtesy of General Counsel Roundtable.

**Figure 1.5**   Problems with Hourly Billing

### AN OVERRELIANCE ON BILLABLE HOURS...

- Does not encourage project or case planning
- Provides no predictability of cost for the client
- May not reflect value to the client
- Penalizes the efficient and productive lawyer
- Discourages communications between lawyer and client
- Fails to discourage excessive lawyering and duplication of effort
- Fails to promote a risk/benefit analysis
- Does not reward the lawyer for productive use of technology
- Puts client's interests in conflict with lawyer's interests
- Imposes on clients the risk of paying for:
  - The lawyer's incompetence or inefficiency
  - Associate training and turnover
  - Adding of time sheets
- Results in itemized bills that report mechanical functions, not value of progress
- Results in lawyers competing based on hourly rates

**The Billable Hour is Bad for Everybody.**

It is a dense list, isn't it? Notice how many of the points relate to efficiency (or lack thereof).

Some inside lawyers understand the fool's goal of getting a law firm to reduce the amount it takes from the client's wallet and decide that reducing spend just can't be done. Those who opt for this approach rarely do so obviously. Instead, the concession to the status quo urges efficiency, more aggressive bill review, and other actions that attempt to rein in outside counsel. Albert Einstein said the definition of insanity is doing the same thing over and over and expecting a different result. These discredited efforts do not provide the game-changing solution needed to meet the "more with less" challenge virtually every law department faces.

At this point, some inside counsel consider value fees, a form of AFA that attempts to tie the fee total to the value received by the client. They try this approach not because they truly believe value fees are the answer but because there is nowhere else to turn. But this willingness to consider value fees raises the question of how to make the transition and ensure the law department gets the game-changing bang needed. How can one avoid the firms that say they're offering value fees when all they are really doing is dressing up their hourly fees? And if the inside counsel doesn't see the expected results, what is the reason?

Those who practice in firms do not have it any easier. The "churn," as *The American Lawyer* calls it, reflects the frequency with which partners change firms, almost always in the quest for "more." The cost to firms is enormous, with guarantees and headhunter fees being incurred before a single dollar is billed. Firms seek higher profits per partner to better their ability to attract lateral partners with significant business, strictly to grow revenue. In April 2013, *Bloomberg Businessweek* reported:

> Every spring, *American Lawyer* feeds the competitive-ness and greed of large law firm partners by posting its annual lists of who's making what. Since law firms aren't required to report their revenue or earnings, *AmLaw*'s intrepid data-gathering draws lots of attention.
>
> The headline news from this year's list: "For the first time ever, neither Skadden, Arps, Meagher & Flom nor Baker & McKenzie heads the AmLaw 100's gross revenue rankings. DLA Piper—already the world's largest firm by head count—is not the top-grossing firm as well."[6]

---

6. Paul M. Barrett, "'American Lawyer' Revenue List Shows New No. 1 Firm: DLA Piper," *Bloomberg Businessweek*, April 26, 2013, http://www.businessweek.com/articles/2013-04-26/american-

Firms make much of this and similar rankings.[7] DLA sent out a press release on the news. But lost in the reporting was the issue of profitability. DLA is *not* one of the most profitable firms. Its focus on revenue speaks volumes about the firm's priorities, and DLA is hardly unique in its priority. Discerning clients should find such focus troubling since it is at odds with their objective of spending less.

Firms focus on *more*.[8] As long as they are not focused on helping their clients do more for less, they are focused on the wrong thing.

---

lawyer-revenue-list-shows-new-no-dot-1-firm-dla-piper.

7. I recognize that this data is about large law firms and many lawyers don't practice in large firms. I share this data not because I am writing for BigLaw or even about BigLaw but because it conveys useful information. If I had similar information about twenty-lawyer firms, I would happily share that as well, but I am unaware of any such data source. This is an example where lessons being learned publicly by larger firms reflect experiences of other firms as well. In my own experience, data rarely reflects what is happening in BigLaw, but it does provide indicia of what clients are thinking in many instances or what strategic opportunities might exist.

8. Not all firms, obviously. But in a competitive world, it is hard to "unilaterally disarm," and as long as most or all of the competition is doing something one way, it is virtually impossible to convince a partnership to take an untrodden path.

# Chapter 2

## DID THE GREAT RESET CHANGE THINGS?

The "Great Reset"[9] in September 2008 appeared to fundamentally change the relationship between clients and their lawyers. Virtually all work done before 2008 was billed hourly at standard rates. In response to the economic catastrophe many clients faced, firms agreed to hold the line on rates, provide discounts, and consider other forms of billing. After 2008, alternative fees entered the lexicon of the profession, and things seemed on the precipice of change. At the fifty-thousand-foot level, the problems with the hourly model were well-known and material and were perceived to be radically at odds with the critical corporate objective of doing more with less. The promise of nonhourly fees appeared equally material and profound.

Change was demanded and seemed to be in the air. But almost six years later, the promise of alternative fees has not been realized. Are alternative fees not the right tool? Was too much expected?

---

9. "Call it the Great Recession, the Great Reset (my favorite), or whatever, the world palpably shook in September 2008 and the repercussions are still very much with us." Bruce MacEwen, "Growth Is Dead: Part 1—Setting the Stage," Adam Smith, Esq., September 4, 2012, http://www.adamsmithesq.com/2012/09/growth-is-dead-part-i/.

A fee arrangement, whatever kind, is just a tool, nothing more. Like a hammer, its use in the hands of a skilled professional will produce an outcome different than if used by an unskilled novice. That conclusion is obvious.

In retrospect, we can see that too much was expected of alternative fees alone. Clients expected that they would be fair and create value. Perhaps firms expected that simply offering alternative fees would be enough; a sort of "if we build it, maybe they won't come" philosophy. It didn't work the way clients wanted or firms feared.

Almost every firm is built on hours. Hourly billing is by definition a zero-sum game. Unless firms change the way they do business, there is no way to avoid the pressure for "more," and the only source of "more" is a firm's clients. The firm builds its profit into hourly rates, so the only way to increase profits is to bill more and hope to collect at least some portion of the higher amounts.

Simply getting more business is not an answer, especially in a tight market. If it was easy get another client so you could bill more hours, every lawyer would do so. But it's not that easy. Rainmakers are the only lawyers who don't have to worry about their hours, and most lawyers are not rainmakers. They have to worry about their billings and collections. So the worker bees bill lots of hours because those hours determine their compensation and, since the Great Reset, often determine their employment status. A system that forces lawyers to choose between their personal well-being and the client's economic interests is not one that will ever yield to the client's interests, and that became even more true after the Great Reset.

The switch to alternative fees prompted by the Great Reset would succeed only if there was a radical change in the way firms generated profit. If clients were going to pay less, the only way for firms to generate greater profits was to reduce the cost of delivering services.

Except for Seyfarth Shaw[10] and a few others, firms have shown little discernible effort to meaningfully lower their costs of production. The easiest benchmark test for determining whether a firm is serious about lowering its cost of production is to examine its real estate and personnel. Lawyers and real estate are the two primary expenses of almost every firm—how can you be serious about reducing costs if you don't address your two biggest cost items?

Because hourly billing is cost-plus billing, for decades firms have had no incentive to radically lower costs of production. They have never learned how to produce results at the lowest possible cost because they have never had to do so. And unless they are moving away from hourly billing, there is little reason to go through the pain of changing the business model. The general absence of material changes in firms' cost of production is evidence of where BigLaw has cast its lot.

But it is poor marketing to tell clients you will not give them what they want, what they need. Big law firms are not poor marketers. So they gave clients what they wanted: alternative fees, at least in name. But what happened in the name of alternative fees was astounding, although obvious in hindsight. Firms had not lowered their cost of production, and partners were not willing to accept reduced profits. Both outcomes could only be accommodated if any alternative fees yielded the same revenue, in the same time frame, that firms would have received if they billed by the hour. So they labeled the expected billable revenue on a given matter an "alternative fee." Said another way, they dressed their billable hour rate in the garb of an alternative fee. A complete charade.[11]

---

10. Seyfarth has made a massive investment in implementing a hybrid of Lean, Six Sigma, and project management disciplines. The hybrid has been named Seyfarth Lean.

11. Obviously not every firm that has used alternative fee arrangements has engaged in this practice. But for the majority, hours continue to be the standard form of billing, and with that comes the pressure of greater revenue with much less focus on the cost of production.

How do we know this? There are three sources of proof:

- Firms compete on revenue. See the discussion about DLA Piper in Chapter 1.
- Clients report dissatisfaction with AFAs because they do not generate enough savings, even though there are enormous savings to be had if AFAs are properly used.
- Firms concede they seek to use AFAs as a surrogate hourly billing.

This last point is stunning. I have had conversations with the managing partners of four AmLaw 100 law firms. In each conversation, the managing partner said that the firm priced a fixed fee engagement by determining how much the firm would expect to bill on the matter under an hourly basis and then converting that number into a fixed fee. Two of the four said a "cushion" was added to protect the firm. Yet another managing partner acknowledged this approach to pricing at a corporate counsel forum at Georgetown University, noting it is all about "how much money comes over the transom before midnight on December 31."

Using fixed fees as a surrogate for hourly billing, or the wolf-in-sheep's-clothing syndrome, is even more egregious than it might appear on first analysis. When clients pay by the hour, they stand to gain if the matter resolves early. Case ends. Fees stop. But given law firms' approach to fixed fees, clients do not gain (from a fee standpoint) if a case resolves early. One in-house lawyer told me he "would be the world's worst businessman to accept such a deal." Is it any wonder clients have become suspicious of these "alternative" proposals from law firms?

Billing by the hour strains the relationship between firms and clients, but the billable hour model is so much a part of law firm DNA that rehabilitation may well be impossible. Absent a full-scale commitment to changing this approach to business, it is unrealistic to expect firms to provide their clients real value. Clients will be forced to continue to engage with their lawyers with one hand firmly on their wallet and a suspicious eye on every special deal offered.

It is fascinating to see the way many clients depict the hourly billing model. In a program titled "Imagine a World without Billable Hours: An Endorsement for Value Based Billing," David Grumbine, senior counsel of Whirlpool Corporation, shared the following list (see Figure 2.1) with his audience:

**Figure 2.1**    A Client's View of the Hourly Billing Model

### DRIVERS SUPPORTING A DIFFERENT APPROACH

- **Case Cycle Time.** The longer a case is open, the more expensive the case. We validated by 10 years of data.
- **Incent Firms to Maximize Efficiency.** Hourly fees are counterproductive to maximize efficiency.
- **Hourly Billing.** Focuses on activities and not value to client. Activities produce more revenue.
- **Cost Predictability.** Hourly budget forecasting is almost always wrong.
- **Communications.** Are negatively impacted by hourly billing.

### GOALS OF VALUE-BASED BILLING ARRANGEMENT

- **Improved Budgeting Predictability.** Fixed Fee Agreements will support better business planning by improved accuracy in financial forecasting and supports risk management objectives to better control costs.
- **Drive Efficiency and Focus.** Firm incented to value time invested as much as client. Motivates focus on outcome of effort, not on the activity.
- **Share in Risk/Reward.** As hourly places 100% of the risk on the client, provide holdback and rewards.
- **Eliminate Communication Blockers.** Hourly billing tends to inhibit communications with firm. Fixed fee should facilitate communications.
- **Pay for Performance.** Incentivize good results.
- **Cycle Time Matters.** Like a wine, a case/project gets more expensive with age and often not better.

**Figure 2.1** (continued)

---

### LESSONS LEARNED AND COLLATERAL BENEFITS

- **Trust.** Critical Requirement. Intent is not to financially squeeze a firm, but to facilitate a partnership. . . A win/win. Never lose focus that the goal is to improve overall results and improve predictability and efficiency.

- **Incentives Work.** Financial rewards for exceeding expectations are a critical component to improving results.

- **Set Cycle Time Expectations.** All of us operate from deadlines. Case in point . . . Impending trial date drives efficiency. Drive cycle time goals to resolve disputes/project completions.

- **Communications and Partnership are Enhanced.** When hourly rates are eliminated, this facilitates communications and enhances teamwork . . . all on the same page.

- **Business Knowledge Improves.** Firms knowledge of business and its processes improve. Firms learn more about the company and processes when the weight of the hourly fees are removed.

- **Employee Time/Involvement Reduced.** Improved business partner knowledge greatly reduces educating firm, rework and hand-holding.

- **Measurement.** Continue to track cost efficiency and results to drive continuous improvement and learn.

---

It is difficult to find a client who advocates in favor of the billable hour. Instead, some voices raise questions about whether alternative fees solve the problems.

Here is the answer: By themselves, they do not. But as a tool used with skill, alternative fee arrangements can make a huge difference—a game-changing difference—in what clients pay for legal services and the value clients receive. To provide value, AFAs must be used with other tools by counsel who have fully committed to the different approach required. In later chapters, we will explore the tools that help make alternative fees effective for both lawyer and client. But first, it is important to know what a real AFA is (and isn't).

# Chapter 3

## UNDERSTANDING THE TERMINOLOGY

The phrase "alternative fee arrangements" raises a question: alternative to what? The obvious answer is "to the billable hour." But lawyers, creative lot that they are, have bastardized the phrase to mean "alternative to stand rack rate hourly billing," meaning that any discount off a firm's standard hourly rates is an "alternative." Interpreting the idea so broadly surely helps a firm's statistics when it brags on how much of its revenue comes from alternative fees. But that kind of statistical sleight of hand misses the point.

Fee agreements promote specific behaviors. For example, billing based on time causes people to spend more time on matters. That fact doesn't change if the hourly rate is discounted, blended, or rack. In a truer sense, alternative fees are about relationships with clients that are not based on how many six-minute increments it took to complete a task. Hourly rate billing is cost-plus billing. In the broadest sense, alternatives are those billing methods that are not cost plus. But to be more precise, here are the definitions I use throughout the rest of this book:

# STRUCTURES THAT ARE NOT ALTERNATIVE FEE ARRANGEMENTS

**Hourly rates.** Clients are billed for the amount of time a given lawyer works, whether in hours, tenths of hours, or some other fraction of hours, multiplied by an hourly rate. Most firms have standard rates, book rates, or rack rates for all of their lawyers.

$$\text{hours} \times \text{rate} = \text{revenue}$$

**Discounted hourly rates.** Clients are billed for the amount of time a given lawyer works, whether in hours, tenths of hours, or some other fraction of hours, multiplied by an hourly rate that is less than the lawyer's standard, book, or rack rate. Most firms will discount hourly rates for many of their larger clients.

$$\text{hours} \times \text{discounted rate} = \text{revenue}$$

**Blended hourly rates.** Instead of using each lawyer's standard, book, or rack rate, a common or "blended" number is used. For example, if the standard hourly rates for lawyers on a matter are $800, $600, and $400 per hour, the negotiated blended rate may be $550 per hour.

$$\text{hours} \times \text{blended rate} = \text{revenue}$$

**Capped hourly rate.** This is the hourly rate billed up to a defined amount.

$$\text{hours} \times \text{rate} = \text{revenue if (and only if) revenue} < \text{cap amount}$$

Why are these *not* alternative fees? All of these fee structures incentivize lawyers working under them to bill more time. More time yields more revenue. As a rule of thumb, if the term "hourly rate" appears in a fee structure, the fee is not an alternative, regardless of what adjective precedes "hourly rate." Discounted hourly rates, blended hourly rates, uncollected hourly rates, or Thursday hourly rates are all hourly rate structures, where more time spent equals more revenue. None of these structures create any incentive, let alone pressure, for efficiency.

I've been on panels with lawyers who have said that blended rates are alternative fees because they are not straight hourly rates, as if any minor deviation from stated rack rates is an alternative. First, a client would have to be stark raving crazy to agree to a blended rate. Firms assign lawyers with the lowest hourly rates to handle these matters. Why? Because firms that successfully utilize low-priced lawyers can achieve realization rates greater than 100 percent. Realization rates are now averaging in the range of 85 percent. Consider the internal value of a matter with realization rates greater than 100 percent.

How do you achieve those rates? As a simple example, say a client agrees to a blended rate of $400. The partner on the matter bills at $600, the junior partner at $450, and the assigned associates bill at $320. If the associates work 100 hours, the younger partner works 20, and the senior partner works 5, that's 125 hours at a blended rate of $400, a total of $50,000. The firm sees this as 100 hours at $320 ($32,000), 20 hours at $450 ($9,000), and 5 hours at $600 ($3,000), or a total of $44,000. The realization rate is approximately 114 percent.

Under a blended rate, firms have two incentives. One is to have timekeepers with rates under the blended amount bill excessive hours; the other is to have lawyers with rates over the blended amount bill as few hours as possible. So clients lose twice: first because the incentive to bill more, not less, is still present; and second because the bulk of the work will be done by lawyers with less experience.

Is it possible capped fees can alter the incentive to bill more? The answer depends on the circumstances. If there is no benefit to being under the cap, what is the incentive to bill fewer hours, at least up to the cap amount? There isn't any. But if the savings are split, the firm is incentivized to bill as little as possible since the savings shared with it are "free money"; that is, fees for which the firm has incurred no cost.

Any rational economic actor should want that free money, right? The answer is "of course," but the assumption that firms act as rational economic actors may be problematic. If a partner's compensation is driven by total billings and not total attributed profit, it may well be in the partner's self-interest to forsake the free money and maximize the total billings, *even if it means exceeding the cap.* Consider a matter with a $1million cap where excesses are paid at 50 percent and savings are shared at 50 percent. If the partner bills $800,000, the firm receives an additional $100,000 (half the amount under the cap), for a total of $900,000. If the firm bills $1.4 million, it stands to be paid $1.2 million. What benefits the partner more?[12]

None of the approaches based on time fundamentally change the behavior of lawyers to the client's benefit. The "more is better" mentality that so infects the legal system is not limited or altered in any meaningful way.

## STRUCTURES THAT ARE ALTERNATIVE FEE ARRANGEMENTS

There is no end to the variety of alternative fees that lawyers and clients can imagine. Over time, a few have come to stand out as being the most used.

**Retainer agreement.** The typical example is when a client pays a standard monthly fee for defined work. It can be in the context of advising clients, so the outside lawyer is available without limitation to inside lawyers or businesspeople to address various matters, such as human resource issues, contracts, and other routine topics. In the

---

12. There are obvious client relationship issues that must be considered in these circumstances, but the example illustrates the simple point that when money drives behavior, not everyone looks at things the same way.

litigation context, retainers are a tool to level off uncertainty. For example, a national retailer sued by landlords but with a long record of early resolution of such claims may find it easier to have a lawyer on retainer to handle these matters from inception to filing written discovery, or to the point of the first settlement meeting, or whatever point of the litigation is agreed upon. *This type of engagement differs from the situation where a client advances an amount, frequently called a retainer, against which future invoices are applied.*

**Fixed fees.** The concept of a fixed fee is simple: a specified sum. But a specified sum for what? It turns out that there are several answers. While conceptually easy, the variety selected makes a big difference in pricing, which is a topic addressed later.

1.  **Portfolio of cases.** If a client has a group of cases or a steady flow of a certain type of case, the client may wish to group the cases. The data for handling prior cases likely shows a range of costs. Fixed fees level the alterations. Consider Figure 3.1 below:

    **Figure 3.1**   Fixed Fees vs. Case-by-Case Pricing

    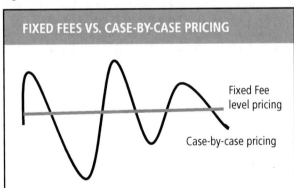

2.  **Single case.** On other occasions, clients have just one case and want to know the price for handling the matter. Single fee for single matter.

3. **Phase of case.** Cases have phases, such as pleadings, written discovery, depositions, experts, summary judgment, trial preparation, and trial. These phases can be priced separately, with a fixed sum determined for each phase. If the phase does not occur (early settlement, a decision not to pursue summary judgment, etc.), the fee for that portion of the matter is not paid.

4. **Single case by time.** Sometimes it is not possible to estimate the fee for a single case because the duration is not estimable. This tends to happen in more complex multiparty cases. In these circumstances, clients and firms can agree to a fixed monthly sum, which is paid as long as the case is active.

5. **Multiple cases by time.** Some clients have a track record that allows them to believe that they will have a certain number (or narrow range) of new cases during a year. A fixed fee for the time period requires a firm to handle the cases filed during a year (or other negotiated period) for a specified sum. As the cases mature into the following year, more certain budgets can be set per case. This approach allows clients the certainty that their budgets will not be disrupted depending on when during the year cases are filed.

For any fixed fee matter, it is common for clients to include a bonus component or holdback to promote behaviors they desire. For example, a client desiring early resolution may pay only 80 percent of the agreed-upon fixed fee (of whatever variety) and pay a declining multiple of the holdback amount depending on how quickly the matter is concluded.

**Contingency fees.** These types of fees are well-known from their prevalence in the personal injury world. This form of payment, recovery of a specified percentage of a defined sum, has become common in corporate plaintiffs' claims. The structure works well when the amount of potential recovery is sufficient to create an incentive for the lawyer to handle the case.

**Reverse contingency fees.** These are similar to traditional contingency fees, but instead are calculated as a percentage of the amount saved for the client who is a defendant in a lawsuit. To work, the base amount from which savings are calculated must be agreed upon in advance between client and law firm. The best circumstances for use are where damages are clear but liability is contested (like a contract claim) or where there were efforts to resolve before the lawsuit was filed and a firm demand from the plaintiff can be used as the baseline.

**Hybrid fee agreements.** In this category, I include the ACES system (employed by Jeff Carr, general counsel of FMC Technologies), capped fees with shared savings, and fee collars.

1. **ACES.** This system requires a budget for an entire engagement at the outset, agreed to by lawyer and client, and it is difficult to change the budget once set. While billing is still done on an hourly basis, the client pays only 80 percent of the invoiced amount as long as the lawyer is under budget. If the lawyer exceeds the budget for a given segment of the case, payment is only 20 percent of the amount over budget. The unpaid balance is put into an "at-risk bucket." At the end of the matter, performance to budget is one of five factors considered in determining whether the client pays the sum in the at-risk bucket plus a multiple of that amount. The budget certainty and the potential premium are the carrots to encourage efficiency, while the possibility of not being paid some or all of the at-risk bucket is the stick to influence desired behavior.

2. **Capped fees with shared savings.** Standard capped fees incentivize lawyers to bill as close to the cap as possible. The add-on of sharing (usually on an equal basis) the amount by which the lawyer comes in under the cap is an incentive to

work more efficiently, since the shared savings are "free money," or in hourly billing parlance, a way to achieve more than 100 percent realization.

3. **Fee collars.** A fee collar sets an amount a lawyer is to be paid. If the lawyer's hours come in on target or at a specified percentage above or below, the fee becomes final. If the hours fall below the agreed percentage under, the savings are shared. If the hours exceed the agreed percentage over, the lawyer is paid only a percentage of the excess amount billed. As an example, a client and lawyer agree the fee is $10,000 with a 20 percent up and down collar, meaning that if the lawyer bills from $8,000 to $12,000, the final fee will remain $10,000. If the lawyer works only $6,000 in billable time, the $2,000 difference is split, and the client receives a $1,000 credit, meaning the final fee is $9,000. If the lawyer works $14,000 in billed time, the lawyer is paid 50 percent of the amount over the $12,000 collar, meaning the final fee is $11,000.

Everyone knows that fee structures incentivize behavior. The real issue with any AFA is determining the behavior that the client wants and then fashioning a structure to produce that outcome. It is not quite that simple, however, because the fee structure is not the only incentive driving lawyer behavior.

Lawyer behavior is influenced, in varying degrees, by the firm's interests, the client's interests, and self-interest. The easiest way to understand this is to examine the plight of associates during the early days of the "great recession," when terminations seemed to be regular events. If associates did not have hours, they might not have jobs, which meant not paying bills, loans, and so on. The pressure to come up with a satisfactory number of hours billed was extraordinary, and no doubt many succumbed and did whatever it took to keep their jobs. While those personal pressures may have lessened, they are still substantial.

Partners operate under their own set of stressors that are independent of the interests of individual clients. Managing partners struggle to keep firms afloat, dealing with pressures created by the profit-per-partner competition among firms and figuring out how to grow revenue to keep pace with growing expenses. One managing partner told an audience at a presentation that his job was "getting money over the transom before December 31." These pressures invariably result in management placing firm interests ahead of those of any specific client and are translated to other partners through the compensation system. Most firms continue to place a premium on total revenue collected rather than the net profitability of any particular engagement.

These varying pressures are not a major hurdle for clients with enormous spend that are the lifeblood of any firm, but they make selection of a fee structure a critical decision for ordinary clients. For that reason, some overlays on fee structures have become standard.[13]

**Holdback.** In this overlay, the client retains a specified percentage of the agreed-upon fee. The holdback accumulates over the course of the matter, and payment of the holdback amount is determined at a set time, perhaps at the end of the matter, when the value of the lawyer's representation is determined in arrears. The amount paid can range from none of the holdback to a fraction or a multiple of it. The factors that determine where on the continuum the outcome falls can be based on defined benchmarks or left to the client's discretion, or they may be a combination of those two. Since my foremost goal is client satisfaction, I prefer agreements that leave the payment to the client's discretion. I believe they force lawyers to pay continuous attention to the client and the client's perception of

---

13. These overlays are most frequently applied to alternative fee arrangements, but that doesn't mean they can't be applied to any other form of engagement.

service quality. However they are calculated, holdbacks are a power-ful tool to drive desired behaviors.

**Bonus.** Bonuses are the same as holdbacks except there is no pool from which payment is made and thus no natural base amount. Bonuses may well be left to the client's discretion where the lawyer and client have a history together. Absent an established trusting relationship, the preferred approach will be to specify at the outset of the engagement any bonus amounts and conditions for payment.

Some in-house counsel worry that a firm will use lesser-quality lawyers or will "lose interest" in a case as the firm approaches the upper end of the fixed fee. At Valorem, we have always suggested to clients that they hold back a portion of our fee to be paid at their discretion at the end of the matter, after our value can be deter-mined. Clients who develop experience with holdbacks learn quickly that firms do not lose interest when there is a large basket of money being held until the end of the engagement.

The other critical factor associated with holdbacks and bonuses is that both encourage a firm to invest additional senior resources in ways that increase the quality of work and the likelihood of a better outcome.

# Chapter 4
## WHAT WORKS WHEN?

Every fee structure has advantages and drawbacks. The challenge is to align objectives with structures. For most clients, the primary goals in most matters are (1) the best outcome, (2) a predictable cost, and (3) the lowest reasonable cost. The third goal is not meant to imply that clients look for the cheapest provider, although a few do, but rather that clients want to ensure they get value for the money they spend. Other objectives may come into play for some clients or in some matters. Figure 4.1 shows different types of fee structures with a few of the advantages and drawbacks of each.

**Figure 4.1**   Advantages and Drawbacks of Fee Structures

| Type of Fee Structure | Advantages | Drawbacks |
|---|---|---|
| **Valuation of Firm Cash Capital** | Encourages client to contact lawyer to secure advice when needed, without regard to cost or administrative difficulties<br><br>Helps avoid problems by getting early "take" on disputes or potential disputes | Unnecessary if inside counsel have significant litigation experience and time to evaluate matters |
| **Fixed fee (general)** | Predictable<br><br>Simple<br><br>Works well with comparable data<br><br>Will increase competition over time, tending to drive down cost | Does not fit easily with current e-billing<br><br>Incentive to be too lean in staffing<br><br>Can generate concerns about inadequate staffing, reduced attention at the end of busy billing periods<br><br>Can generate concerns about windfalls if quick wins obtained<br><br>Can lead to dissatisfaction with work/fee relationship if there are scoping errors |
| **Fixed fee (portfolio)** | Predictable<br><br>Built-in savings for client if fee set correctly<br><br>Reduces administrative burden on client<br><br>Allows client participation on more strategic level<br><br>Deepens law firm knowledge of client | Requires time and effort to assess portfolio—must be balanced<br><br>Must be clear on staffing so the portfolio does not become a way station |

**Figure 4.1**   (continued)

| Type of Fee Structure | Advantages | Drawbacks |
|---|---|---|
| **Fixed fee (time period)** | Covers defined time periods<br><br>Assists in budget management in face of potential uncertainties<br><br>Encourages client to use firm<br><br>Encourages firm to identify creative ways to avoid disputes/litigation or to resolve quickly | Could be considerable variance in workload<br><br>May be some client concern that firm gets windfall for slow periods<br><br>Hard to calculate fee amount |
| **Basic contingency** | Avoids cash drain<br><br>Incentivizes firm to focus on outcome<br><br>Works best with high damage, uncertain liability profile | May eliminate pursuit of claims with low or uncertain damage amounts<br><br>Can lead to overpayment for risk taken in a good liability and damage case<br><br>Can cause client to "overpay" when successful, relative to other fee structures |
| **Defense contingency** | Works well for cases with fixed damage amounts but uncertain liability<br><br>Works well where there was firm bid/ask resolution numbers before suit filed | Same as for basic contingency |
| **ACES** | Creates firm budgets and a holdback/at-risk component<br><br>Incentivizes efficiency | Risk of "gaming the budget" that requires in-house counsel to be diligent in budgeting process |
| **Fee collars** | Addresses concerns about fairness of fee relationship to amount of work | Still links value of work to amount of work and time spent doing it |

Each of these structures can be modified to allow pieces of one to fit with part of another. For example, it is very common to use a reduced fixed fee arrangement in concert with a partial contingency fee. Firms like this modification because it minimizes risk. Clients like this modification because it prevents the runaway 33 to 40 percent contingency awards that are customary under that fee structure while reducing short-term outlay.

Beyond these structures, there is the overlay of holdbacks and bonuses. Holdbacks and bonuses, if sizable enough, are insurance against any concerns about lack of effort. These structures also allow the client the chance to determine the total fee *after* the outcome of the case, when the value of the legal services can best be judged. Outside counsel have expressed fear that because outcomes are out of their control, they might provide great service but still lose a case. Thus they are loath to risk any portion of their fee.

It is hard to debate this view, and, candidly, I have no interest in doing so. The core of this objection is that what the lawyer is selling is time, and time is unrelated to outcome. I don't believe that lawyers should sell time, but my opinion is wholly irrelevant. Clients, as the buyers, have to judge whether they are buying time or buying outcomes. Those who buy outcomes will welcome the concept of a portion of the fee being held back.

The other value of a holdback is that it feeds the client service commitment that is the cornerstone of effective value fees. When the client retains control over the award of a holdback or bonus, it is a substantial incentive for outside counsel to ensure that the client is fully engaged and pleased with the work. The incentives work exactly as they should to promote quality, efficiency, and effective and timely communication.

With the range of possible fees available, I am frequently asked which structure is best. Fixed fees, combined with a holdback or bonus, have been the best alternative for Valorem and its clients. That said, we have engagements using nearly all of the structures discussed above. But in operating a small business, the value of predictable revenue is hard to overstate. It allows us to plan and to focus efforts on areas that we can leverage for greater future value and challenges us to work more efficiently so we can maximize our profit margins. At the same time, the holdback or bonus causes us to remain focused on what is important—outcomes and meeting our clients' defined objectives.

This leads to the question of whether the fee should be fixed for an entire case, a part of a case, or a group of cases. As shown in Figure 4.2, the smaller the piece for which the fee is fixed, the harder it is to lower the fee.

Likewise, when there is greater certainty of the amount of the fee, there is greater value in the fee (see Figure 4.3). This is because certainty is a value to firms, at least to smaller firms, and that value can be shared with the clients. The exchange between certainty and value is a fair one.

Clients are understandably reluctant to create significant long-term obligations to a law firm. But since an engagement can be

**Figure 4.2**   Value and Fixed Fees

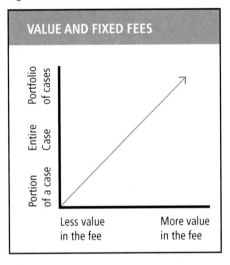

**Figure 4.3**   Value, Certainty, and Fixed Fees

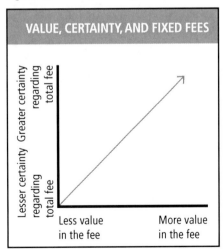

terminated at any time if the firm does not perform, a client interested in seeing the maximum value from an alternative fee should bundle work together in a way that creates predictable cash flow for the firm. Performance can—and should—be incentivized through a holdback program. Clients must understand how firms arrive at their fees, however, since many firms resort to analyses of estimated hours times rates to come up with fixed prices. Fees created through this analytical framework are not true alternatives; they are hourly rate fees with different labels, and they fail to provide real value.

There are numerous ways to structure fee agreements. While hourly billing has been the default, today many lawyers and clients are interested in exploring alternatives. The key in fashioning an alternative is to focus on the lawyer behaviors that the client wants to incentivize, cognizant of risks that may accompany those behaviors. The creation of an agreement places a premium on upfront discussions between lawyer and client.

# Chapter 5
## SO WHERE ARE WE NOW?

Law is always changing. It just does so slowly. William Osler, one of the founders of Johns Hopkins Hospital and considered to be the father of modern medicine, said that "the search for static security—in the law and elsewhere—is misguided. The fact is security can only be achieved through constant change, adapting old ideas that have outlived their usefulness to current facts."[14]

In the 1980s, good lawyers were those who knew the law. That was all that was required for success. Slowly, business judgment became a necessary additional attribute. Consider this evolution of the profession during the past three decades (see Figure 5.1), provided by Nancy Jessen of Huron Consulting.

The demands for efficiency and predictability were growing before the Great Reset but have now become commonplace. The notion of consistent delivery has emerged only recently.

---

14. http://thinkexist.com/quotation/the_search_for_static_security-in_the_law_and/150088.html

**Figure 5.1**   Evolution of the Legal Profession (1980s–now)

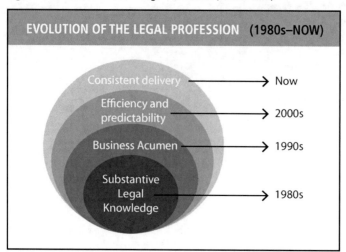

What does this mean? It means change is happening more rapidly than before. We have moved through the efficiency and predictability phase into the consistent delivery phase in five years. This mirrors the increasingly rapid pace of change in the world at large, which Ray Kurzweil and others predict will accelerate. One author writes:

But you cannot even begin to get your head around the present without understanding the accelerating, exponential rate of change itself, both in technology and how that impacts human life and society, including politics and government.

Change is inevitable and there's not a damn thing you can do about it—except figure out a way to deal with it for yourself.[15]

The change curve in Figure 5.2 shows the ever-increasing pace of acceleration.

Lawyers being lawyers, there is a compulsion to debate the slope of the curve, but that misses the point. It is beyond debate that this

---

15. Glynn Wilson, "On the Accelerating, Exponential Rate of Change in Society," *The Locust Fork News-Journal*, January 16, 2011, http://blog.locustfork.net/2011/01/how-do-we-deal-with-all-this-change/.

curve, whatever its slope, exists. There is great change in our world. Businesses are fully cognizant of it. Law departments are growing faster than law firms because companies are changing incredibly fast to survive in a tough global marketplace. That has led to a growing gap between law departments and outside lawyers (see Figure 5.3):

This widening gap between law departments and law firms in how much and how fast they are changing contributes to the strain that exists between many in-house counsel and outside lawyers.

**Figure 5.2**   Change Curve

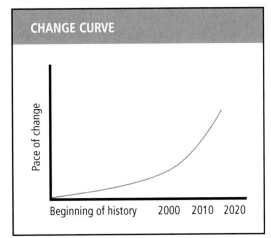

**Figure 5.3**

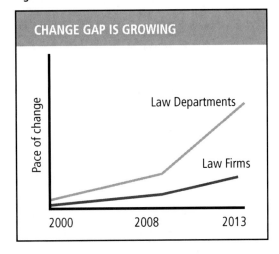

Where are we going? The renowned Richard Susskind has offered a compelling view of the future in his two most recent books, *The End of Lawyers?: Rethinking the Nature of Legal Services* and *Tomorrow's Lawyers: An Introduction to Your Future*. He explains why and how work will move from mostly bespoke, or custom, to packaged and commoditized. Ancillary to these changes, new service models will develop, including third-party providers, such as legal process outsourcers, and use of off-shore resources, along with the growth of technology for lawyers. Susskind believes that clients will play an even greater role in driving reducing amounts paid to law firms as work is automated or outsourced with greater frequency.

Paul Lippe,[16] the CEO of Legal OnRamp, has offered the view shown in Figure 5.4:

**Figure 5.4** Law: Past, Present, and Future

|  | Law Classic | Law Today | Law Becoming |
|---|---|---|---|
| **High level value** | Expertise | Relationship | Outcomes |
| **Orientation** | Conflict, complexity, individual | Uncertain | Effectiveness, teamwork |
| **Information** | Scarce | Overwhelming | Ubiquitous, processed |
| **Professional identity** | Objectivity | Risk manager | Architect, information manager |
| **Metrics** | Responsiveness | Responsiveness, cost savings | Anticipation, alignment, outcomes, value |
| **Process** | Reactive | Uncertain | End to end |
| **Tools** | Brain, pen | Email, word processing, e-billing | Brain, Network, shared environment, collaboration |
| **Key innovation** | Re-framing substantive law arguments | Organizational structure | Systems design |
| **Bumper sticker** | "Leave no stone unturned" | "What do you want me to do?" | "Let's design a solution together" |

---

16. Paul is my co-columnist for the *ABA Journal* online column The New Normal, and he serves on Valorem's advisory board. His insights on the changes in the profession have informed a great deal of my thinking.

We know where we have been. We know the future will be different—most likely significantly different—from the present. The question is what that future looks like. If hourly billing is not the road to the future, something else is. In trying to determine that "something else," I am guided by the belief that answers may be found in the business world where clients exist.

Many claim that law is a profession and use that notion to excuse all manner of sins. Regardless of how valid that claim is, the *practice of law* is a business. While some believe this has not always been true, it now is indisputable (except for those who continue to dispute it). One need only think of the cartoon of an ostrich doctor telling his ostrich patient, "Take two aspirin and stick your head in the sand." D. Casey Flaherty, a visionary in-house counsel for Kia Motors, shared a slide (see Figure 5.5) with the audience at a law firm he recently visited:

While the debate whether law is a business or a profession was fun, it's over. Lawyers and law firms are subject to the same immutable rules as regular businesses and the same lessons those businesses have learned over the past hundred years. Ask law department leaders how their companies price the goods they sell: "Fixed price." "Turnkey." Similar ideas are the norm. None of us get to spend as much as we would like. People operate within a universe of constraints and uncertainties.

**Figure 5.5** "You Are Not Special"

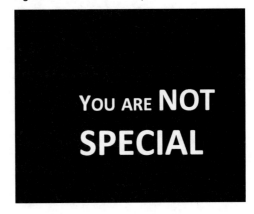

You can join the ostriches with their heads in the sand, or you can figure out how to operate in a competitive world that is becoming more so every day. The future is not the hourly rate. The future is not any one thing. The only certainty about the future is that it will be complex and varied. There will be no single road. Different clients will prefer different arrangements, and some will prefer different arrangements for different matters.

# Chapter 6
## ISSUES CREATED BY AFAS

Many who contemplate or experiment with alternative fee arrangements, whether as clients or firms, raise issues that continue to link service to time. Those issues need to be confronted directly.

## "WE WOULD HAVE MADE MORE IF WE BILLED HOURLY."

Not every value fee matter will provide heroic profit margins for the law firm. These episodes generally result in partners criticizing those who agreed to take the engagement for an alternative fee, and the criticism usually includes the lament above. Implicit in this statement are the assumptions that (1) every hour would have been billed (2) at standard rates and (3) the firm would have realized 100 percent of what it billed. These assumptions ignore reality, but more significantly, they disregard the largest assumption—that the firm would have been hired to handle the matter even if it hadn't agreed to use a value fee. These days, many clients will refuse to engage with firms unless on a nonhourly basis.

When a firm uses alternative fees—that is, fees that are not based on the number of hours worked—there is an irresistible impulse to compare the final amount paid by the client with the amount the firm would have made if it had billed the client by the hour. That comparison usually incorporates the assumption that the firm would have billed its standard rates and the realization would be 100 percent. At Valorum, we went through a period where we made these comparisons. It stopped after a client (also a friend) heard me make that analysis and said simply, "You wouldn't have gotten the matter if you billed by the hour, so there's no point to the comparison." Every firm that uses nonhourly fees for the bulk of its revenue eventually realizes this—the comparison with hours-based revenue simply is not relevant.

The foundation on which this realization is built is that pricing is not an exercise in figuring out time. Many managing partners or pricing partners of large firms have stated (mostly privately) that the number of expected hours for an engagement, along with the rates associated with those hours, is the basis for fixed fees offered by their firms.

The standard equation for hourly billing is:

$$\text{hours} \times \text{rates} = \text{revenue}$$

The hours-focused firms base their fixed fees on this formula:

$$\text{expected hours} \times \text{expected rates} = \text{fixed fee}$$

Visually, this fee proposal looks like Figure 6.1:

**Figure 6.1**   Hours-Based Fixed Fee Proposal

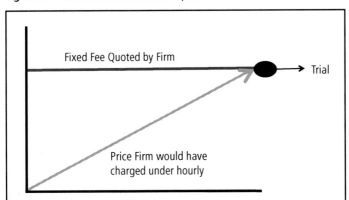

The hours-based fixed fee is hourly billing dressed in different clothing. An in-house lawyer who rejected a proposed fixed fee calculated in this manner, only to hear the firm say that the "client didn't want alternative fees," told me, "I'd have to be the worst businessman on the planet to accept that deal." He explained that under an hourly arrangement, if the matter resolved early by motion or settlement, he paid only the fees incurred. Under the firm's proposal, if the matter resolved early by motion or settlement, he still had to pay the full fee. There was never a point at which the client "won." In Figure 6.1, the space between the red line and the orange line represents risk previously borne by the firm that, in this fee model, is transferred to the client. Clients are too smart to accept that.

Usually, clients turn to nonhourly billing to achieve predictability *and* lower total cost. If a firm is at all responsive to its clients' needs, the normal measurements are immediately out of whack. A fee lower than that expected under an hourly rate engagement will result in a lower realization number. Realization is the percentage of revenue collected from the total billable amount (total hours × standard hourly rates). Everyone with experience in law firm finance knows that a lower realization number is not a positive.

To achieve the lower prices clients seek, lawyers and firms must change the metrics used to determine the quality of engagements. Time becomes far less relevant than in the old model, where it is the measure of "productivity" (the notion that more time is more productive could only happen in law). The new measure of productivity is results obtained. The cost to the firm to obtain those results is the benchmark for determining the profitability of an engagement.

To illustrate the concept, let's use the example of Bob and Mary, both senior associates. On the first of the month, they are asked to prepare motions for summary judgment on cases that are of the same degree of complexity and value. Mary works 140 hours in that month to achieve the result (the final brief), while Bob works 190 hours for the same output. The cost to the firm is the same for both associates. Even if Bob had to work 220 hours, the *cost* to the firm is still the same because his hours are not a variable cost. If the firm's bonus program is based even in part on the number of hours worked, the firm's message is that it values Bob's efforts more than Mary's. Of course, the right outcome should be to value Mary's efficiency more, since it creates the opportunity to do additional work and generate more revenue for that period.

If the preceding example occurred in an alternative fee environment, the disparity between Bob's hours and Mary's would not create more revenue for the firm. That Bob may have generated additional revenue under an hourly model would be irrelevant to the profitability analysis. The hourly billing system shows a disconnect between lawyers' traditional definition of "productivity" and the meaning of that term in the business world, which underscores the distance between legal business analysis and business analysis. That distance does a disservice to law firms and creates needless acrimony in lawyer-client relationships. It also teaches Bob and Mary the wrong lessons about how to provide the best service to clients.

The most pressing challenge for law firm leaders who see the importance of aligning their firm with their clients is to identify every way in which the firm uses billable hours as a measure of performance. How ingrained in law firms is the hourly model? Name a firm that doesn't use hours billed as a basis for associate compensation and advancement. Budgeting is driven by estimated hours. Realization rates, significant in partner compensation, are based on application of standard hourly rates. Some firms are starting to look at profitability of clients and matters, but that practice remains the exception. And only a handful of firms are truly serious about creating efficiencies in practice. Were firms truly concerned about driving down the cost of producing results, effort in this area would be much more pronounced.

One afternoon at a recent conference, large name-brand firms extolled the benefits of new software that better captured time spent on various matters, promising higher billing for no new work. That was hardly music to the ears of the in-house lawyer sitting next to me. A lawyer from one name-brand firm decried the need for professional project management, noting that the partners could figure it out on their own. Of course, if they actually can figure it out on their own, one can only wonder why they have not yet done so. Here was another case of a lawyer claiming the lessons learned by real businesses could be ignored by law firms.

Law firms *are* businesses. Many stubbornly cling to the notion that because law is a profession, law firms are not subject to the demands of every other business. The solutions businesses have developed that could address problems law firms are experiencing should be a starting point, not dismissed because the solutions did not originate in the legal field. The fact that more revenue could be earned through a different billing methodology should be as irrelevant to lawyers as the fact is to automakers that they could make more money if they priced vehicles by the pound. They don't price that way, so they don't waste time thinking about what would happen if they did!

## "PLEASE SEND ME SHADOW BILLS."

Few words in the "value world" cause more consternation. After agreeing to a fee structure and fee, some clients want to see "shadow bills," reports that show each lawyer's time, hourly rate, and work done in a given month or other period—the typical support that accompanies an invoice based on hours. The time records may contain UTSB task codes.

There may be many reasons that clients want to see shadow bills, but generally two are proffered: (1) to make sure necessary work is being performed in a timely manner and (2) to make sure the law firm does not receive a windfall, which would be perceived by a client as a bad deal.

The knee-jerk reaction is to give clients what they seek. And in the end, that may well be the preferred course. But it is not the best first response, which should be to ask why a client wishes to receive shadow bills and to engage in discussion about the reason.

If the client suggests shadow bills will help track work performed, the response may be to agree it is important for the client to know what work is to be performed *before* it is performed, by whom it will be performed, and when the work should be completed. This "work plan" approach allows the client the comfort of knowing what is to be done *before* the fact. A later report can confirm the work was performed as planned. This approach is much superior to the client reviewing a shadow bill, since bills are sent weeks or months after the work is completed, eliminating any possibility of the client providing corrective direction. It also bears noting that bills are hardly designed to be easy-to-understand reports that actually show what work has been done.

For clients who simply want to follow the work performed, this usually suffices. But some use the "follow the work progress" rationale to hide their concern about the profitability of the engagement to the law firm. At the risk of being unfair, I've never heard of a client expressing concern that shadow bills were necessary to make sure the firm wasn't making enough money, only that it might be making too much.

The client concern that the firm may make too much is the counterpoint to partners' concern after an engagement that the firm would have made more if it billed by the hour. Both concerns tie value to hours and entirely miss the point of using value fees in the first place.

Imagine this scenario. A few weeks after the lawyer and client agree to a $100,000 fixed fee for an entire case, the lawyer calls the client and says that the opposing counsel has agreed to dismiss the case. The client understandably wants to know the details, and the lawyer explains that she spent a lot of time culling through the documents and found some very favorable evidence. She contacted the opposing lawyer and shared her findings, convincing him he had no case.

The client is thrilled with the outcome but realizes that the outside lawyer spent only fifty hours on the case, which at a normal rate of $500 per hour would be $25,000. The client does not want to pay the full $100,000 fixed fee.

What is the lawyer to do? Should she call her adversary and suggest the case be reinstated so she can do some discovery and "earn" her fee? Would that make the client happier? The simple answer is this: It was worth $100,000 to the client to have the matter handled, and a highly favorable outcome was obtained, so the client got the desired value—the outcome—and thus should pay the agreed-upon fee. The old adage about not learning how the sausage is made may well apply.

The client must understand how this "unhappiness" with the profitability of the engagement will impact future behavior. Some outside lawyers would refuse to work with the client again. After all, if the parties cannot trust each other on the fee, the foundation for the relationship is, to say the least, shaky. And if there are future engagements, there may well be different behavior. The outside lawyer may not invest time that early again, since doing so resulted in no greater profit and a loss of revenue. The answer, of course, is that the client, like the lawyer, should focus on the outcome, not on the amount of time to obtain it.

This scenario illustrates the importance of trust between lawyer and client. One critical objective of AFAs is to change the focus of client and lawyer from time spent to result achieved. Results are unrelated to time, so it should not matter to either side how long it takes to secure a result. If a client balks when a result is achieved quickly because it would have been cheaper to pay an hourly rate, it is only natural that the outside lawyer, who would have made more under hourly billing, will want reciprocal protection. In such a circumstance, the focus has shifted entirely back to time, and there was no point to using the AFA in the first place. Everyone needs to understand that a fee based on results will compare sometimes favorably and sometimes unfavorably with a time-based fee for the same matter. No one should expect to be a winner in these comparisons every time.

Once the trust issue is addressed, there are three compelling reasons the parties should eschew shadow bills.

A. Value is not about time. Remember, the focus is results, not hours—as agreed at the outset of the engagement. After all, aren't we trying to get away from time determining value?

B. Timekeeping costs money. Your firm's leaders should want to forgo costs that do not contribute to outcomes. If they don't, they are not demonstrating the right mindset for maximizing the value of fixed fees.

C. Invoices are a lagging indicator for the information provided. A better practice is to forecast work so that it is planned and executed with assent of the client.

# "WHAT DOES A VALUE FEE ENGAGEMENT LETTER LOOK LIKE?"

Every matter begins with an engagement agreement, or at least it should. An entire book could be written on engagement letters and how law firms write them in such a one-sided fashion as to be off-putting for clients. Some clients refuse to sign any engagement letter other than their own form. Recognizing the many issues that arise in engagement letters of any kind (advance conflict waivers, anyone?), it is important to understand the issues that relate to use of alternative fee agreements.

  A. **Set a specific fee structure.** Determine the nature of the fee structure: fixed fee, fixed fee with holdback, capped fee, capped fee with shared savings, or some other structure. If there is any kind of holdback or bonus element, specify that the client will determine whether it is paid or the criteria that will be used to determine how much of the holdback will be paid. You need to be cognizant of some basic accounting issues, which are addressed in Chapter 16. For any type of retainer engagement,[17] the agreement should specify when the law firm will recognize the payment as revenue.

  B. **Define staffing.** Clients are concerned that firms may use less experienced or less qualified lawyers and staff once a fixed fee has been set. Avoid the problem by defining in writing which lawyers and paralegals will be used on a matter and what their respective roles will be. If Jane is the senior lawyer, it is important to define her role as "lead counsel" (or some other suitable term for being in charge on all aspects of the matter) rather than "strategic advisor," meaning that

---

17. A retainer engagement is not the same as a financial retainer that is a deposit or prepayment of fees that resides in a lawyer's trust account until an invoice is generated and applied against the retainer deposit.

someone else will be handling the case and Jane will provide only oversight.

C. **Specify amounts of payments and when fees will be billed and paid.** Most firms using fixed fees identify advance payment, rather than payment in arrears, as a benefit. The benefit is lost if the client pays bills on a sixty-day or longer cycle, unless you consider that by timing the submission of your bills. The preferred approach sets the timing of bills and payments at the outset of the engagement. It also is important to specify whether fees will be billed monthly, by some other period (predetermined phases), or by work completed (an incentive for firms to work faster). Amounts to be billed need not be equal, so specifying the amounts that will be billed, when they will be billed, and when payments will be made eliminates any potential misunderstanding.

D. **Specify the assumptions on which the fee agreement is based.** There are general assumptions built into every fee agreement, including the likely volume of documents, the issues (broadly defined, such as "no counterclaim"), the likely number of depositions, the time frame of events, number of witnesses, time to trial, and so forth. All assumptions underlying the fee structure should be specified.

E. **Specify all work to be performed and any work not to be performed.** All work to be performed should be specified. For example, anticipated or possible motions should be defined as included or not. It is common to include one discovery dispute but not more than that, since discovery disputes are frequently within the control of the client. It is equally important to define any work *not* included. For example, if the firm believes it will be doing significant document review but the client anticipates outsourcing such work or if such reviews were completed on an earlier case, the expectation that such work is not part of the fee agreement should be specified.

F. **Identify the criteria for change order approval.** If the outside firm believes circumstances have changed materially, it will submit a change order proposal. Not every change order must be approved; the client always has the right to accept the risk of not changing the scope of the engagement. But it is important to clarify the criteria that the client will use to determine whether or not the work identified in the change order is within the original scope of work. Was the issue or circumstance foreseeable? If so, the change order is not appropriate, and the work should be performed under the previously agreed-to fee structure. Of course, if the client requests some additional service, there should be agreement on how the extra work will be compensated.

G. **Require the client to approve any spending outside the fee agreement.** The money being spent on fees and disbursements is the client's. The client has the right to determine if, when, and how such money is spent. Funds for experts, vendors, and other expenditures over an agreed-upon threshold should require advance approval.

H. **Require early case assessments (ECAs) and updates.** For many clients, this is a condition of payment of any fee. They want to invest in the prosecution and defense of the right cases, and ECAs are critical tools in deciding which cases are worthy of investment. In fact, it is entirely reasonable to create a specific fixed fee for ECA investigation, which will be followed by a more fulsome fee agreement once risk has been assessed and a strategy determined (see Chapter 8 for more information on ECAs).

I. **Address basic what-ifs.** Certain things can be planned for—for example, a key member of the team leaving the firm, significant scheduling changes, interlocutory appeals, or bankruptcy of your adversary. It is helpful to note in an agreement that if these types of things occur, the parties will discuss renegotiation of the fee if necessary.

J. **Specify whether local counsel fees are included or excluded.** One rule of thumb is that local counsel fees should be included if primary counsel is responsible for selecting local counsel and has the power to replace them. This gives primary counsel the control to ensure that local counsel fee budgets are followed. If the client chooses local counsel, primary counsel probably will propose that local counsel fees not be included in the fee agreement. Whatever is decided, the engagement letter should address the issue.

K. **Specify whether expert fees are included or excluded.** Some clients request "all in" numbers from their lawyers, while others anticipate that expert fees will be the subject of a separate agreement at an appropriate time. There are pros and cons to each position, but the engagement letter must address the issue.

L. **Be clear about whether fees for trial and trial preparation are included.** Most cases settle, so if fees for trial are included in the overall fixed price, it will be terribly inflated. If you know a case is likely to be tried, you can build in the price of trial as a separate phase. Frequently, it is easier to estimate the cost of trial when you are to closer to trial because the factors influencing price are likely to be more certain. Either way, be clear about whether the fee agreement includes trial and at what phase of the process the fee agreement ends.

M. **Consider whether a general retainer agreement providing volume discount is in place.** The client may have a general retainer agreement with some firms providing a volume discount based on the total fees paid in a year or some other period. In this situation it should be specified whether or not the engagement governed by an alternative fee arrangement is included in the general retainer agreement providing a discount. It sometimes may be appropriate to specify how the alternative fee arrangement will be included in the general retainer agreement. Some portions or all portions of the fees could be included or excluded. For instance, the base fee could be included in the calculation of the volume discount provided for in the general retainer agreement, but the bonus element might be excluded. All components of fees could be included or excluded. As always, effort should be made to eliminate any potential misunderstanding.

Regardless of fee structure, the best engagement letters reflect detailed discussions that lead up to the engagement and reflect the terms of the parties' agreement. Full disclosure is always the best practice. The terms discussed are important for an alternative fee engagement letter, but counsel using such a fee structure should add whatever additional terms are believed necessary to have the best understanding with the client.

The key takeaway is the lesson Albert Einstein once shared: "We can't solve problems by using the same kind of thinking we used when we created them." The ruthless truth is that there is an hourly rate mentality in large swaths of the legal profession. Many lawyers compare everything that is not hourly with that system and then express discomfort with any difference. The point is that there have to be differences. The focus must be on outcomes, not the time it takes to achieve them. Without a change in our focus and our benchmarks for evaluating performance and value, we will simply default back to that which many clients find unacceptable.

# Chapter 7

Standing alone, alternative fees do not save money for clients or provide greater profit for law firms. There is plenty of evidence, discussed earlier, that many firms use estimated hourly fees as a basis for determining fixed fees. One reason they do this is that they do not have systems and processes in place to help them reduce the cost of producing results. Firms operate under the same basis profit calculator as all other businesses.

The formula is profit = revenue (price) − cost. Under the hourly model, shown in Figure 7.1, as the law firm's cost (hours) increases, so does the price to the client. But under the fixed fee model, shown in Figure 7.2, the only way for the firm to increase profits is to reduce the cost of generating outputs.

**Figure 7.1**  Hourly Fee Model

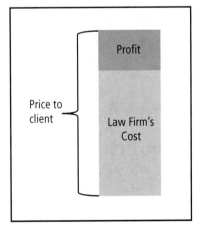

53

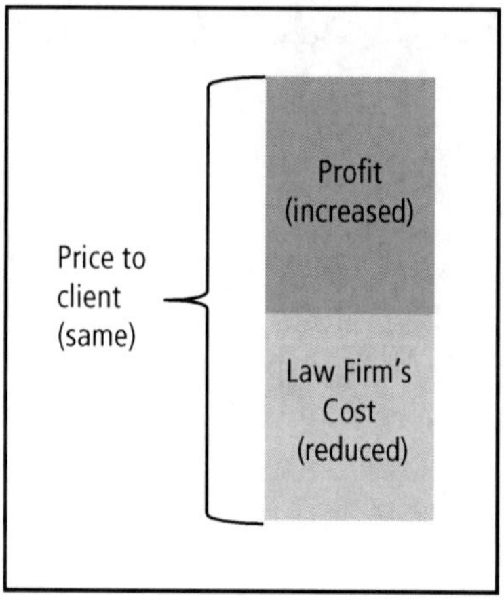

For firms, the issue is how to reduce the cost of production. But clients must ask the same question because they need to know what their firm *should* be doing and, to the extent they want to be true partners, what they should be working on together with the firm. The objective is to lower the cost of production on the matter under consideration, which can lead to lower prices on future matters.

**Figure 7.2**   Fixed Fee Model

Both firms and clients must share in the value generated by reductions in the cost of producing results.

Figure 7.3 shows the tools that are designed to lower the cost of production.

Books have been written about each of these tools, so it would be a fool's errand to try to provide a complete discussion here. When I was studying contracts in law school (it seems like forever ago!), my professor took pains to explain that we would spend more time learning contract law when we had our first case than any student would ever spend in law school learning the topic. He was right, and copying his wisdom, my message is that those who choose to use alternative fees will spend considerable time becoming adept in the use of the tools discussed in the next few chapters. The key is to understand the important role these tools play in helping lawyers drive down the cost of production (thus increasing their margins).

**Figure 7.3**    Tools That Lower the Cost of Production

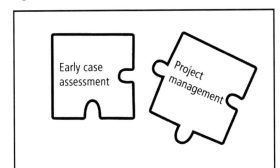

# Chapter 8
## EARLY CASE ASSESSMENT

When you accept the premise that no business has the resources to fully and limitlessly defend every case, you necessarily introduce the concept of allocation of limited resources. Some cases get more, some less. Making well-informed decisions early allows better allocations to be made.[18] Resources are spent where they generate the greatest return.

The concept is simple, yet all too often, substantial sums are spent before the client knows the full extent of the risks a case poses. The extreme example is the settlement on the courthouse steps, after all of the transaction costs, including trial preparation, have been incurred. Fred Bartlit, the iconic founder of Bartlit Beck, refers to "the letter." He means the letter the client receives from the law firm very late in the case saying the client should pay a substantial amount to settle the case and avoid trial, all because facts were learned in discovery that have caused outside counsel to reevaluate the viability of the client's position at trial. Of course, a huge sum already has

---

18. Early case assessment can take many forms, and each client must determine the level of information wanted and the level of uncertainty that will be tolerated. But the concept of quickly gathering the essential information and evaluating it in a systematic fashion is a rock-solid tool for making better decisions early in the litigation process.

been paid to the law firm by the time the letter is sent, and it is the first time the firm has seen fit to recommend a settlement of the amount contained in the letter.

The real problem is this: Whether due to financial incentives or not, it appears that many lawyers apply far greater critical thinking at later stages of a case (see Figure 8.1).

**Figure 8.1**  Critical Thinking Curve in a Case

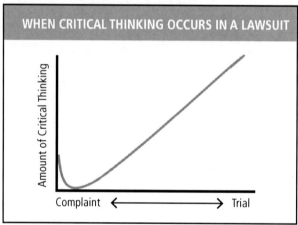

WHEN CRITICAL THINKING OCCURS IN A LAWSUIT

Amount of Critical Thinking

Complaint ⟵————————⟶ Trial

In other words, lawyers think about a matter at the beginning, but they really focus on the adversary's case and then become far more critical as the case nears trial. By delaying the deep critical thinking until this later date, they do not discover the flaws in the client's position early, which too often causes improper evaluation and unjustified investment.

While early case assessment (ECA) is not a new idea, rigorous early case assessment is rarely practiced. With aggressive early case assessment, the critical thinking curve would appear as shown in Figure 8.2.

Spending more time thinking and analyzing at the beginning of a dispute means making better decisions about resource allocation, strategy selection, tactics, and execution. The challenge is how to get the most out of early case assessment.

Those who excel at ECA know it is not as simple as hearing your client contact relate the essential facts of the case. The features of a good assessment are

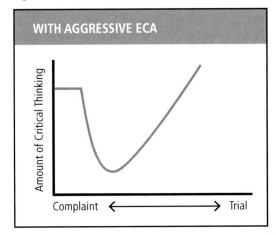

**Figure 8.2**   Critical Thinking Curve with ECA

1. interviewing the important witnesses, including challenging the story a witness tells;

2. analyzing the documents that relate to the essential issues in the case; and

3. assessing relevant business dynamics.

While there is general agreement on these features, execution is frequently lacking. Many times, in-house lawyers hear from one person involved in the dispute who tells the business unit's story and sends along a few chosen documents to support it. The story and the documents are passed to outside counsel for an early case assessment. Too often, though, the story is accepted at face value. No one explores gaps or challenges details, particularly in light of the story contained in the documents.

Decades ago, business was conducted by telephone calls and in-person meetings. Sometimes letters were sent, but the bulk of the information came from witnesses. Today, a substantial percentage of business occurs via e-mail and text messaging and digitized data that is shared. The volume of any person's communications dwarfs what it used to be, which challenges a person to fully and accurately remember what was said, by whom, and when. Thus, the corpus of facts has moved from people to documents. Witnesses frequently are needed only to verbally tell the story found in the documents.

What happens in many early case assessments? Documents are essentially ignored, save for the self-selected ones chosen by people who may well be trying to recast the story. A significant percentage of the time—perhaps as much as 50 percent—the story changes completely once document review is completed, and in almost every case, the other side's story becomes much clearer.

These two phenomena mean that an aggressive ECA requires collection and review of a large enough volume of documents that "bad" facts are likely to be revealed. Witnesses also must be interviewed—or reinterviewed—once the preliminary document review is complete. Because one should always try to avoid duplicating work, the sequence should be to accumulate documents, review them, and then talk about them with the right individuals.

Contract cases provide a classic example. The client may give you the contract and tell you "what happened." E-mails may well reveal that the parties agreed in writing to alter the contract terms or that a certain course of conduct was accepted or even suggested by your client. These e-mails can change the assessment completely.

An aggressive early case assessment is not always cheap, and there is a tendency to do the work in-house. But some in-house lawyers are too busy to do a thorough ECA, some are not comfortable challenging their business unit clients, and some lack the experience of cross-examining witnesses. While many in-house lawyers are as capable as their outside counterparts, errors can come into play, as shown in Figure 8.3:

**Figure 8.3**   ECA: Indirect Process

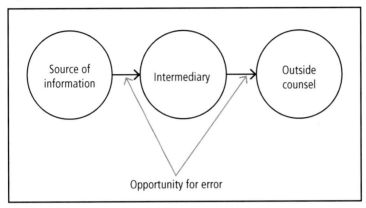

Instead, the most effective means of obtaining information is direct, as shown in Figure 8.4:

**Figure 8.4**   ECA: Direct Process

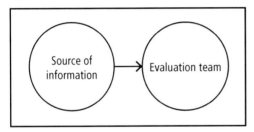

Notice the change from outside counsel alone doing an evaluation to an evaluation team. As in all aspects of work in the new normal, the goal uses teams to collaborate in producing outcomes. Here, the team would include inside and outside counsel. The direct process removes one chance for error, one filter between information and judgment.

The mindset of many is that the ECA is simply a hurdle to jump en route to "handling the case." In the new normal, ECA is the most important part of handling the case because it allows the best decisions to be made sooner rather than later. Early decisions are essential to maximizing allocation of scarce resources.

I have included a form for an ECA in the Appendix.

# Chapter 9
## PROCESS MAPPING, PROJECT MANAGEMENT, AND CHECKLISTS

It has been said so many ways by so many extraordinarily successful people:

> *"Amateurs practice until they can get it right;
> professionals practice until they can't get it wrong."*
>
> —Popularized by Harold Craxton, a professor
> at the Royal Academy of Music in London

Tom Peters @tom_peters 12m
Some of you say I should use this
word or that. Fuggetaboutit. My word
Train. Train. Train. Train. Train. And
then train some more.

Tom Peters @tom_peters 27s
JWooden's remark about being good
practice coach leads to all important
point: Training can be off-the-charts
fantastic. Settle for no less.

Tom Peters @tom_peters 8m
JWooden/training: "I wasn't much of a
game coach, but I was pretty good
practice coach." BWalsh/training:
"The score takes care of itself."

Tom Peters @tom_peters 5m
Larry Bird on the epitaph he'd like:
"He played as hard at practice as in
any playoff game." (approx)

> —A series of tweets from Tom Peters

> *"It's not the will to win that matters—everyone has that.
> It's the will to prepare to win that matters."*
>
> —Bear Bryant, legendary football coach at the University of Alabama

What shall we take from these formidable speakers? To succeed at an act, one must repeat it . . . again and again and again. One must learn to perform the act flawlessly at all times so when pressure is great, the act is still performed flawlessly. How does this play into law? Into alternative fees?

Volumes have been written about process mapping, project management, and related efficiency efforts like Lean and Six Sigma.[19] No common nomenclature has really emerged, though some have been drawn to the term "legal project management." A little background is in order.

**Six Sigma** focuses on improving quality of outputs by identifying errors in input and then focusing on developing processes that eliminate the errors. With respect to products, it is an outcome where 99.9999998 percent of the items are statistically expected to be free of defects. The same percentage would apply to steps or processes in a service environment, depending on the output contemplated.

**Lean** focuses on the creation of value for the customer and is based on the belief that anything that does not create value for the customer is waste, which should be eliminated. Lean has been applied to the service environment. The wastes in service are delay, duplication, unnecessary movement, unclear communication, incorrect inventory, opportunities lost to retain or win customers, and errors in the service transaction itself.

**Kaizen** is a Japanese philosophy that focuses on continuous improvement—learning from mistakes so mistakes are not repeated. It also means every aspect of a business is under constant evaluation to determine how it might be improved.

---

19. Among the references available to those interested in these topics, two of the top choices are Jim Hassett's *Legal Project Management Quick Reference Guide,* Third ed., 2013 (http://www.legalbizdev.com/projectmanagement/quickreferenceguide.html) and a list of many resources on Pam Woldow's blog, *At the Intersection* (http://www.pamwoldow.com/category/legal-project-management/).

From these three ideas, **Lean Six Sigma** emerged. This concept focuses on eliminating waste and providing goods or services at a rate of 3.4 defects per million opportunities.

When Lean Six Sigma is applied to law, the following activities emerge as the essence of discipline:

1. Determine the steps you will take to do something, either by reviewing what you have done before or analyzing a matter anew.

2. Put those steps in the most efficient and effective sequence.

3. Practice 1 and 2—make them part of your DNA.

4. Determine before doing the work the time and resources that will be devoted to a given task.

The sequence in which tasks are performed matters. Take, for example, learning the facts as the plaintiff in a case of corporation versus corporation. How does a lawyer typically accumulate relevant facts? Figure 9.1 lays out the process.

**Figure 9.1**   Typical Method of Accumulating Facts

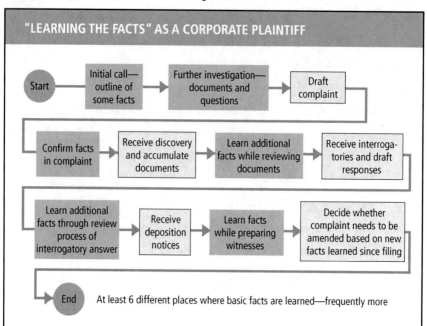

This sequence makes no sense on several levels. First, there is great repetition of work effort. This is wasteful, as illustrated in Figure 9.2.

**Figure 9.2**   Wasted Time in the Work Effort

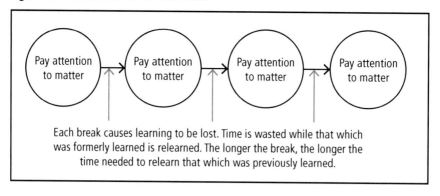

Second, the sequence results in learning significant information after the complaint is filed and after many key decisions have been made. Instead, a design like the one shown in Figure 9.3 is far preferable.

**Figure 9.3**   A Better Way to Accumulate Facts

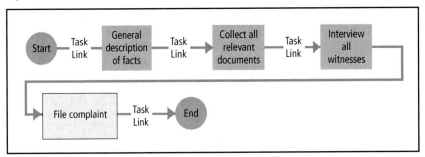

Imagine approaching a plaintiff's case like this: In sixty days (obviously the time could be longer or shorter as required), you accumulate and review all of your client's documents, interview all available witnesses, and prepare and file not only the complaint but also all of the documents you expect to produce and responses to all reasonably expected interrogatories. You demonstrate strength at the beginning, and you accomplish related tasks simultaneously to extract waste from the system. I believe this would lead to not only cheaper litigation costs but also more effective litigating.

Since sequence can play such an important role, you need to start by identifying the sequence you (or your firm) follow for a wide variety of tasks. Based on the experience of many who have completed this exercise, there probably is a significant variation between what you *think* the sequence is and what it *actually* is. What it actually is must be determined by involving everyone in the exercise of process mapping, from secretaries and paralegals to senior trial partners. There are stories of a lawyer saying something like, "The document comes to me. I review it and give it to the next lawyer" while the lawyer's secretary explains that "you get it electronically and then ask me to print it for you, which I usually have to do twice because you lose one copy on your desk, and then you ask me to type in the changes you've marked on the hard copy," and so on. At virtually every stage, there are likely to be many tasks no one person thinks about.

The next step is to come up with the right sequence. I don't mean for a single sentence to suggest this step is easy. It isn't. It is highly fact specific and may well warrant involving an expert to assist. But it is the next step.

Fred Bartlit of Bartlit Beck has frequently compared the sequence that Bartlit Beck lawyers employ to prepare expert depositions with how it was done at Kirkland & Ellis when Bartlit was the top trial lawyer there. At Kirkland, and I suspect at most firms, someone lower on the food chain on a case team prepares an outline, which is then pushed up the chain and edited and redone until it comes to the senior lawyer, who frequently reworks the entire outline. Why does this happen? Because the people preparing the initial drafts have little experience in the courtroom, little experience deposing experts, and perhaps little experience deposing anyone. Using this sequence persists for economic reasons.

Bartlit Beck and firms that have learned from it, or perhaps learned on their own the hard way, know that it is far more efficient for the senior lawyer to prepare the first draft of the deposition outline and then ask for comments. Whether to object to discovery or answer it is frequently influenced by the lead lawyer's expectation of how the case should be tried, so the senior lawyer should be involved in a discussion, however short, about the approach to responding to discovery. The right sequence eliminates waste and improves output.

After the right sequence is agreed upon, the critical next step is using it or practicing it until it becomes part of the unconscious mind. Ray Bayley, formerly the global head of outsourcing for PricewaterhouseCoopers and now the CEO of Novus Law, explains this with an experiment where he asks a person to say the alphabet:

ABCDEFGHIJKLMNOPQRSTUVWXYZ

(average: 8 seconds; 100 percent accuracy)

But then comes the hard part. Bayley asks the person to say the alphabet again, backward:

ZYXWVUTSRQPONMLKJIHGFEDCBA

(average: 50 seconds; about 80 percent accuracy)

Same alphabet and a known sequence, but doing it one way takes six times as long, with material differences in accuracy. Why is that?

The answer is forthcoming, but let me offer another illustration many of us share. I experienced this phenomenon when teaching my kids to drive. Experienced drivers "just know what to do." For most of us, driving is effortless—we know when to turn. For my kids, it was anything but effortless; in fact, they seemed to put great effort into making mistakes and scaring the bejesus out of me.

After capturing his audience's attention with the alphabet demonstration, Ray Bayley uses neuroscience to explain why we can't say the alphabet backward as quickly as we do forward and why it wasn't my kids' fault they began their turns slowly.

When you start learning something, it is in your conscious mind.[20] At some point, the process moves to your unconscious mind. I've seen it with my teenage drivers. Professional musicians know when they can perform a piece flawlessly without thinking about each note or finger movement. Bricklayers know how to lay a brick perfectly every time, automatically. And so on. Things go from our conscious mind to our unconscious mind.

Why is this important? Our unconscious mind operates hundreds of thousands of times faster than our conscious mind. You need not think about something—you can just do it. There is plenty of data showing how many times you must repeat an action before

---

20. I am not a neuroscientist, and this discussion reflects nothing more than a layman's understanding of complex scientific analysis. I include examples to illustrate the principles as I understand them.

it becomes habit—that is, moves to the unconscious mind. So it makes sense to get tasks into the unconscious mind if you want them to become automatic.

Document review provides a great example of the role that process plays in litigation. The analysis of the content of a document is substantive, but recording judgments made about a document (what it's about, is it privileged, etc.) is process. Not having to think about what needs to be done as part of the process measurably speeds up the review and enhances quality.

The same is true for virtually every task. Sequence matters. And when we learn the right sequence and follow it every time, we increase the speed with which the process is completed and reduce the chance of error. Even substantive tasks like brief writing and responding to discovery have processes associated with them. For example, does the total cost of writing a brief depend on whether the first draft is prepared by a senior partner or a young associate? It turns out it does. It costs much less to have the senior partner prepare the first draft or the first outline of a key deposition.

Planning matters. We live in a world of case budgets and fixed fees, so it is critical to ensure that resources and money are spent only on the right matters, and then only in an amount relative to the importance of a given issue. Writing a long brief on a low-value case where the judge is unlikely to read the motion before it is presented is a waste.

Thus the need for legal project management. In the *Legal Project Management Quick Reference Guide*, Jim Hassett of LegalBizDev identifies eight key issues in legal project management.[21] The bracketed notes are my additions to his thoughts.

1. Set objectives and define scope. [Know what the deliverable looks like.]

---

21. http://www.legalbizdev.com/projectmanagement/quickreferenceguide.html

2. Identify the steps to complete the task and schedule them.

3. Assign the tasks.

4. Plan and manage the budget. [The budget could be money or time—"x must be done by Tuesday."]

5. Assess risks to budget and schedule.

6. Manage quality. [If the budget does not allow elite work, how do we determine "good enough"?]

7. Manage client communication and expectations. [This is critical at the outset of a project, particularly where "good enough" is the target for work—you want your client to understand and agree.]

8. Negotiate changes of scope. [This could be brief writer negotiating with lead partner, or lead partner with client.]

Why are process mapping and project management so important? Because these are the tools used to drive down the cost of producing an outcome or a deliverable. Clients have a right to expect this even on an hourly basis, but firms using a cost-plus system (hourly billing) have zero incentive to reduce costs this way (and perhaps some disincentive). But if a firm fixes its fee, failure to properly manage a project reduces its profit.

Some people argue that they do custom work and say project management only applies to repetitive commodity work. The fallacy of this argument is plain. Every case, no matter how bespoke, contains elements of process and is composed of numerous projects that need to be managed properly. Few clients would be pleased with a lawyer who sends every colleague and paralegal off to handle a matter with a "spend whatever it takes" directive. The truth is that *all* projects are managed—some poorly, some well, and still others by neglect. So the issue is not whether there should be project management. There should, and the case for it is overwhelming.

The case for process mapping and project management is so compelling that all clients should ask their firms how they have implemented these two concepts. Why is the question important? Firms need to make a healthy profit. Clients want a fixed fee that lowers their cost. To achieve profit, a firm must manage its work to lower its cost of production. If it doesn't do so, how is it going to provide a lower price *and* make a healthy profit? It can't. Any guesses on who loses in that scenario?

The last piece of the efficiency puzzle is checklists. Everyone is familiar with to-do lists—reminders of projects or tasks you need to complete. Checklists make sure you do the right things in the right order at the right time. The best explanation for the importance of checklists is found in *The Checklist Manifesto: How to Get Things Right* (Metropolitan Books, 2009). The author, Atul Gawande, is not some lightweight. He is an associate professor of surgery at Harvard Medical School and an associate professor at the Harvard School of Public Health. He leads the World Health Organization's Safe Surgery Saves Lives program. *The Checklist Manifesto* is one of the most significant books I have read, and it became mandatory reading for my colleagues.

Why are checklists so important? Litigation occurs in nothing less than a maze of rules. Lawyers study rules in law school—civil procedure, rule of evidence, the substantive rules. We have federal rules, state rules, local rules, and rules issued by individual judges. In some states or jurisdictions, failure to follow even the most insignificant rule can wreak havoc on a case. I recall sitting in a courtroom in Los Angeles for three hours watching a judge consider matter after matter. In the three-hour period, she did not decide a single matter of substantive law. Everything argued and decided related to a claimed violation of a rule or procedure.

Checklists are *great* for ensuring that rules are followed.

Lawyers also practice in a world where there are so many things going on simultaneously that it is possible to forget something. We do some things infrequently enough (such as trials) that it is hard to remember all the issues that can arise.

Checklists help avoid shortcomings in these areas.

Figure 9.4 shows a portion of a five-page checklist created at Valorem for final pretrial conferences, the ones where all the jury selection and other trial issues are being addressed:

**Figure 9.4**  Partial Checklist for Final Pretrial Conference

| Issue: Jury Selection | Explanation |
|---|---|
| Determine number of jurors to be seated for trial | |
| Determine number of alternates to be seated | |
| Determine if verdict must be unanimous | |
| Trial time estimate—push low | This relates to the number of days the jury venire will be told to expect the trial to last. Most trials are shorter than expected, but critically most employers will pay for no more than 10 days of jury service. If trial estimate is longer, many employed potential jurors will we excused. |
| Number of prospective jurors on the venire brought into court | |
| Determine if court uses juror form. If yes, determine availability of completed forms | Some courts allow lawyers to obtain copies, sometimes for a fee. *Have check available.* |
| Determine how court selects prospective jurors from the venire panel to populate the jury box for questioning. Random or sequential order. | Critical to determine if you can tell "who's next" from jurors not sitting in jury box. |
| Number of prospective jurors to be seated in the box at one time | |
| Number of prospective jurors to be questioned at one time | |

**Figure 9.4** (continued)

| Issue: Jury Selection | Explanation |
| --- | --- |
| Obtain number system for jurors seated in jury box | |
| Confirm whether voir dire by lawyers allowed? | |
| Rules on using juror names? | |
| Confirm no exhibits shown during voir dire | |
| Confirm no discussion of case specific facts | |
| Any rules on scope of questions allowed | |
| "Good for goose/gander" rule? | If one side starts asking questions of a certain type without objection, does that mean that the other side can ask same types of questions without objections being sustained? |
| Number of preemptory challenges per side | |
| When and how will for cause challenges be considered? | What order? Outside the presence of the venire? Before peremptory challenges? |
| Are preemptories announced to the jury or to the court? | Do you have to stand up and say "We would like to thank and excuse Juror Number ____"? |
| Does the court permit strike backs? | For a detailed discussion of this issue, see http://www.juryblog.com/the-trial-lawyers-rights/right-to-back-strike/ |
| Are alternates selected separately? | Do they know they are alternates during trial? |
| Additional preemptories for alternates? | |

**Figure 9.4**   (continued)

| Issue: Jury Selection | Explanation |
|---|---|
| Request pre-instruction to entire venire that:<br>• Do no speak to parties or lawyers until case is over<br>• Do not perform any research on the internet, or elsewhere about the issues, the parties or the lawyers<br>• Not permitted to speak to lawyers<br>• Not permitted to speak to each other or others about the case | |
| Rules for voir dire? | Speak from seat or stand? Movement allowed? |

Much more is included in the full checklist, which is found in the appendix.

Some topics that are appropriate for checklists include the following:

- notices of motions
- certificates of service
- signature requirements for responses to requests for admissions
- signature requirements for responses to interrogatories
- verification of completeness requirements for production of documents
- procedures for videotaping depositions
- preparation of audit response letters

There are many other areas for which checklists are extremely useful. If you think about what cases you handle and where, it is possible to develop a comprehensive list of such checklists.

Process mapping, project management, and checklists are the tools you should use to make sure you do the right things the right way every time and aren't using excessive resources for the particular task at hand. They are the tools that help the client (and you) know that the investment of resources in a given task or matter is appropriate and consistent with the client's desires for resource allocation.

# Chapter 10

## DECISION TREES

At some point in almost every case, someone has to determine how much the case is worth from a settlement perspective. How much is a fair amount to pay? How much is a fair amount to accept? Some lawyers rely on a gut feeling, and others engage in a more analytical approach. Sometimes the decision is easy. For example, if A sues B to recover a liquidated sum of $100,000 and the chance of winning is 50 percent, analysis suggests that both sides should identify $50,000 as their settlement value, one side paying and the other side receiving. Because real-life litigation is rarely so simple, however, lawyers and clients look for different ways to determine the value of cases being litigated.

The first problem is the language of "odds." Lawyers tend to use phrases like "good chance of winning." I once participated in an exercise where both in-house and outside lawyers were asked to write down the percentage chance of winning they ascribed to the phrase "good chance of winning." For outside lawyers, the range was from 20 percent to 70 percent. For inside lawyers, the range was from 50 percent to 90 percent. A 70-point range is hardly effective communication. Imagine being the outside lawyer who meant 20 percent and whose client heard 90 percent!

The next problem is multiple points of decision that can influence outcome. How does one determine value if there is a 25 percent chance that the judge lets in a crucial piece of evidence, but the outcome based on that decision is vastly different? Imagine there being multiple such decision points, as is common in patent cases.

The good news is that there is a solution to both problems: a decision tree. The better news is that most people at U.S. corporations are familiar with this tool (trees are used routinely in business schools and many businesses). Following are some examples of decision trees. The first (Figure 10.1) relates to the simple illustration at the beginning of the chapter—a 50 percent chance of winning $100,000.

**Figure 10.1**   Decision Tree: 50 Percent Chance of Winning $100,000

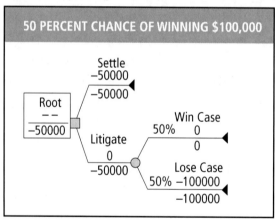

Figure 10.2 is a tree analyzing a demand of $25,000 in a personal injury case.

**Figure 10.2**   Decision Tree: Analysis of Personal Injury Case

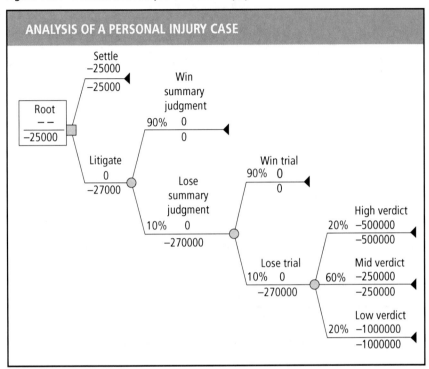

Figure 10.3 is a tree created to value a combined breach of agreement not to hire a contract worker and copyright infringement claim.

**Figure 10.3**  Decision Tree: Value of Combined Claim

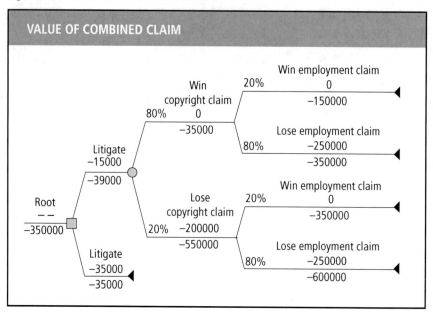

Hopefully the examples show the importance of the concept. The trees were easy to create using commercially available software.[22] The software does the math to provide an outcome value based on the lawyer's evaluation of various outcomes, the cost or benefit of each outcome, and percentage likelihood of each possible outcome.

Some businesses use the decision tree outcome values to establish reserves, others use them to determine settlements, and still others use them to establish benchmarks for determining outcome success.

Trees are very important tools, but they are also a great way to communicate with clients. When the CEO of a client company was presented with a tree in a very complex case, he raved about it because it was a tool with which he was familiar and because the

---

22. These trees were created using DecisionPro software from Vanguard Software Corporation. DecisionPro has been updated and is now Vanguard Studio.

percentage allocations were easier to understand than the lawyer language of odds ("good chance") that he normally was provided.

A decision tree is not meant to be a substitute for informed judgment. It is a tool that informs judgment.

# Chapter 11
## TOWARD AN UNDERSTANDING OF RISK AND SPEND

For many years, the whiteboard in my office contained this message:

**WHAT DIFFERENCE DOES "IT" MAKE TO THE OUTCOME?**

"It" was circled a dozen times. This was my reminder that on a fixed fee case, everything we do has a cost that reduces our profit margin. There was no rule we could not do "it." There was a rule we darn sure had to think about why we should do "it."

The message is no longer on my whiteboard because thinking about "it" has become second nature. If you consider this further, there may well be better ways to ask the essence of the question: What value does it bring to the case?

However you choose to ask the question, it is incumbent to challenge your thinking about everything you do so that only essential value-adding or value-preserving steps are taken. You will be surprised how many things fail to meet the benchmark you set.

Doing less than everything on a case carries risk to the client. Clients get that and they are comfortable with the idea. They are at ease discussing risk and deciding what risks are worth taking. They live in a world of limited resources, so they make risk decisions every day, deciding when to spend money and when to settle, where to spend and where not to spend. We as lawyers don't have the unilateral right to not do "it," at least with most clients. But clients do expect us to identify the option not to do "it" and the risks and benefits that accompany the decision.

Two things have become clear in the past five years. First, it is amazing how much fat there is in most litigation. Lawyers have gotten used to doing things in the name of certainty that just don't need to be done. Second, clients are growing ever more comfortable operating in a riskier environment. Multibillion-dollar business decisions are routinely made based on less certain information than outside lawyers demand before they will predict the outcome of a case. Inside lawyers now realize they pay a huge premium for that certainty and that making decisions with less information is often prudent business practice.

These risk conversations are a critical part of value fee arrangements as both lawyers and clients look to do only the work that most influences the outcome of a case. If outside lawyers are not asking to have these discussions, the odds are they are not looking aggressively at ways to do only what is required on a case and nothing more.

Doing less is one critical way of lowering the price to the client as well as lowering your cost of production. There is no rule that 100 percent of the savings should go to the client, but those who don't share such savings substantially with clients ought to remember the old saying "Pigs get fat, hogs get slaughtered." There is no rationale that justifies the client paying the same for greater risk. Meanwhile, what incentive does the lawyer have to do less, since doing so may well hurt the chance of achieving certain performance benchmarks? The answer is to share the savings.

# Chapter 12

## DISAGGREGATION

For every task, someone must decide who will perform it, and there are usually several different choices. What criteria are used for the decision? I believe that each selection should be driven by the answers to the following questions:

1. Who can perform the task at an acceptable level of quality?

2. Of those identified in number 1, who can perform the task most cheaply?

3. If more than one option emerges from number 2, who can perform the task the most quickly?

The answers to these questions are sometimes surprising. For example, one of the most expensive parts of any case is the review of documents, both the client's and the opposing party's. Too often, firms simply take over the review task for financial reasons—they make oodles of money doing document review—and out of a narcissistic belief they can do it better than anyone else.

In several areas, the answers to the questions are data driven. And when it comes to many expensive tasks, the correct answer is that the law firm option does not provide the highest quality or the best value for the client.

Document review is a good example since it is one of the most costly aspects of any lawsuit and it is process intensive. The client must accumulate all relevant documents, which under the Federal Rules of Civil Procedure and most state court rules provides for an extremely broad collection. There are a variety of e-discovery tools available to reduce the size of the pile of documents that ultimately must be reviewed and analyzed.

Once the pile of documents is created, someone must learn what is included. Enter document review. Document review is not just deciding relevance. It includes determination of privilege for the client's documents. But it also involves analysis of all parties' documents, development of a chronology, preparation of witness files for deposition, determining which documents are needed for filing or responding to motions for summary judgment, and ultimately preparing witness files for trial.

Document review has become one of the most important parts of every case. When I started practicing law in 1982, much of the communication that told the story of the case took place in person or over the telephone. As a result, witnesses held much of the story of the case. Now a huge percentage of communications occur electronically, and the volume of communications handled by any one individual is much higher, meaning witnesses' recall of specific events is less. As a result, the story for most cases is found in the documents. Uncovering that story swiftly is a significant element in making better decisions early in the matter.

Document review is a process. It can be engineered. A highly engineered process necessarily tracks quality and how fast results are delivered, among other things. The engineering of a process is not something that comes naturally to lawyers. But lawyers loved to do the review process because historically it was a "body dump." The strategy was to put a lot of young lawyers in a room and let them sort the documents. The expense of this strategy was breathtaking.

Clients complained, so firms started using contract lawyers instead of their own associates, but they marked up their cost of engaging the contract lawyers, and thus the price to clients remained high. Finally, nonlawyer enterprises entered the picture and drove the costs down significantly.

I have looked at many third-party document review vendors. In my experience, Novus Law provides outstanding quality and value. This is a matter of opinion, which is driven by exposure, so it is entirely possible that other vendors offer similar value. But Novus is a compelling illustration of the importance and value of disaggregation.

The founders of Novus are not lawyers; they are instead serial entrepreneurs who have mastered outsourcing. One thing they learned is that every "touch" or "step" in a process has an error rate. They studied document review and found the following (Figure 12.1):

The high cost, poor quality, and slow process opened the door to process improvement. What if one change was made: doing privilege review at the same time as traditional first level review? The results are shown in Figure 12.2.

One small change provided minor but measurable improvement in quality, speed, and cost. This led to the idea of doing a more thorough review at the initial stage. Novus designed its "one touch" system and obtained the results shown in Figure 12.3.

**Figure 12.1** Accuracy, Delivery, and Cost in Document Review

## ACCURACY, DELIVERY, AND COST IN DOCUMENT REVIEW

| | E-Discovery Vendor | Contract Lawyers/LPO | | Law Firm | | | | The Story |
|---|---|---|---|---|---|---|---|---|
| | Data collection/ processing | First level review | Second level review | Privilege review/log | Witness files | Key issues / documents | Order of proof outline | |
| Accuracy | | 99% | × | 99%³ | × | 99%³ | × | 99%³ | × | 99%³ | × | 99%³ | × | 99%³ | = | 86.2% |
| Delivery | | 43.5 Sec | + | 21.0 Sec | + | 2.5 Sec | + | 3.8 Sec | + | 6.0 Sec | + | 7.3 Sec | = | 84.1 Sec |
| Cost | $.05 | + | $.97 | + | $2.04 | + | $.26 | + | $.39 | + | $.65 | + | $.80 | = | $5.19 |

Poor quality
Slow process
High cost

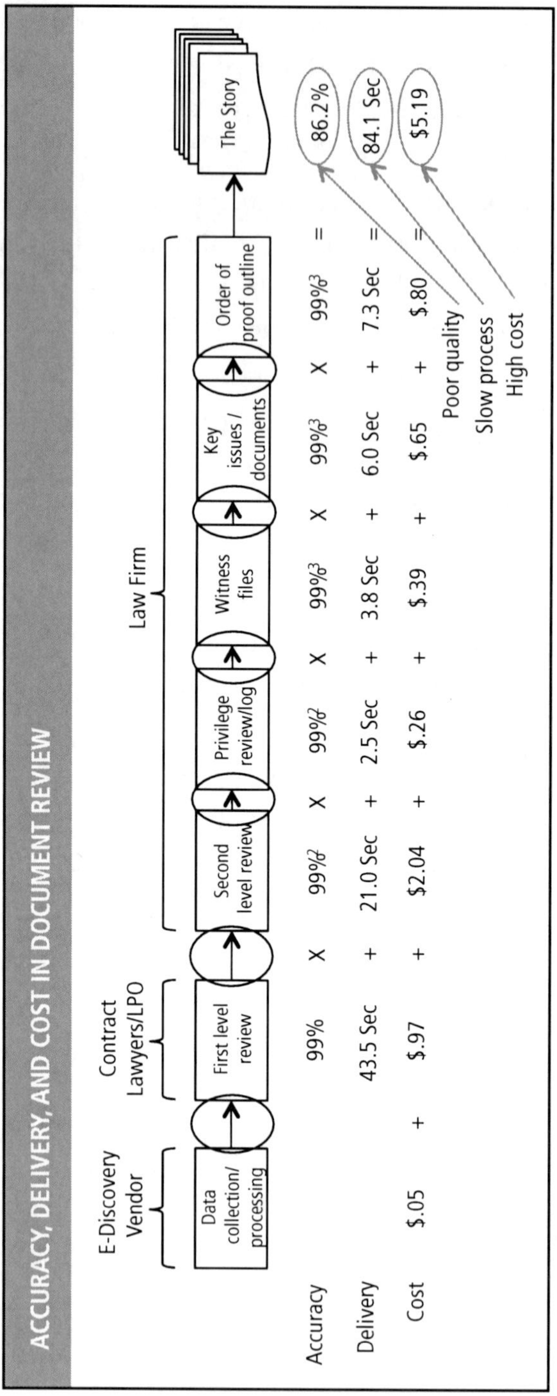

**Figure 12.2**  Accuracy, Delivery, and Cost with Privilege Review

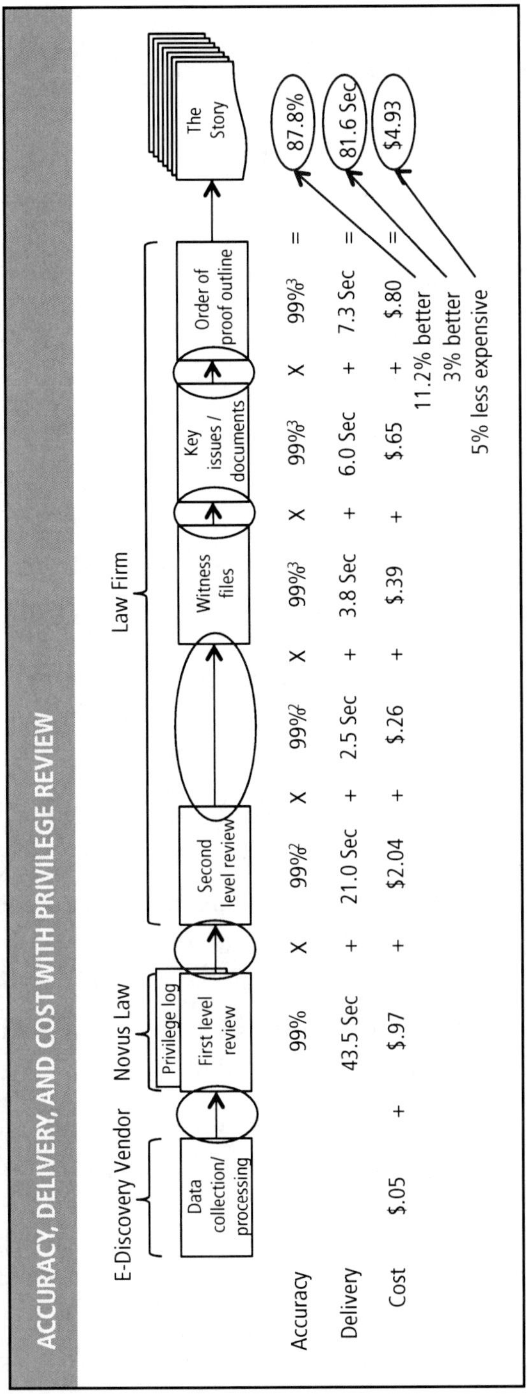

**Figure 12.3**   Novus's One-Touch System

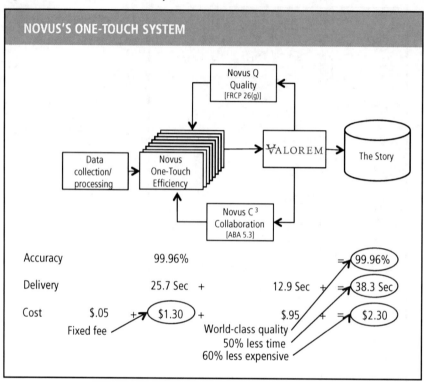

The Novus-engineered system achieves better quality faster, at a fraction of the expected cost. One Novus client, Deanna Johnston, vice president of litigation at Fireman's Fund Insurance, has found that Novus's approach saves Fireman's Fund 15 to 30 percent on cases that average $3 million in fees. That is 15 to 30 percent of the total cost, not just document production.[23] Novus's CEO estimates that clients save $3 in payments to law firms for every $1 paid to Novus.

I believe these numbers do not reflect the full potential Novus provides.[24] First, the time to knowledge is materially improved. As

---

23. Rachel Zahorsky and William D. Henderson, "Who's Eating Law Firms' Lunch?," *ABA Journal*, October 1, 2013, http://www.abajournal.com/magazine/article/whos_eating_law_firms_lunch.

24. I write about Novus because I know the company well and am comfortable with the value it provides. I do not mean to suggest that there are no other entities providing the same value; I just haven't found them.

a result, both counsel and client can make informed decisions earlier, better utilizing resources. Deposition preparation starts at a much more advanced level and consumes essentially no time for associates and paralegals and also does not include the savings associated with reviewing the production by other parties. As radiated throughout the entire case rather than just the document review portion, the Novus effect is profound.

This is one example of savings achieved through disaggregation that inures to the benefit of the client. There are others, and more emerge all the time. For instance, if a company like Novus masters the content of documents early, there is no reason it cannot provide the information needed for responses to interrogatories under Rule 33 of the Federal Rules of Civil Procedure, particularly Rule 33(d) (1), which requires a party to "specify the records that must be reviewed in sufficient detail to enable the interrogating party to locate and identify them as readily as the responding party could."

As use of technology increases and the number and nature of alternative legal service providers proliferate, it is incumbent to always ask yourself if someone else is better at a particular project than you are or can do the same or better work for less. In a case requiring many people to be interviewed, I'd rather have the interviews done by a retired cop or FBI agent who interviewed people for a living than by a lawyer with no "field" experience. I would rather have complex financial fraud documents reviewed by a forensic accountant than by a lawyer. Among the few things lawyers do that require a law license: appear in court, sign pleadings, take depositions, and render legal opinions. Virtually everything else can be done by nonlawyers. Find those nonlawyers that offer value and do excellent work and use them. In this regard, a lawyer has to act like a general contractor, subcontracting work to great professionals in each area rather than trying to do everything as a jack-of-all-trades but master of none. The client deserves that enhanced quality and savings, especially when master tradespeople are cheaper.

# Chapter 13
## AFTER-ACTION ASSESSMENTS

When lawyers become concerned about the cost of producing results, they also need to focus on how to get better at producing great results at even lower costs. Remember, the less something costs relative to a fixed fee, the greater the profit margin. Two critical questions that must be asked after every engagement are "What did we do well?" and "What lessons can we learn so we are better next time?"

These are not novel questions. By now, you know I believe that lawyers do well to look outside the profession to see how others have met the challenges lawyers face. In this era, there is no more effective team than the Navy SEALs. The fact that every mission ends with a debrief, also called an after-action assessment, speaks volumes. Writing for *Forbes* in September 2012, former Navy SEAL Brent Gleeson identified the debrief as one of the important elements of SEAL success:

One of the things that really builds camaraderie in the SEALs is that we can always count on our fellow team members to tell us when we screwed up! There is always an after action review or mission debrief . . . always a review of the tough lessons learned from each mission. *This is how we have constantly improved our tactics.* [emphasis added] In the same way, successful business leaders learn as much from their failures as their successes. But as long as you collect the right intelligence and properly apply what you have learned to the next situation, you can ensure more successes than failures down the road. . . .

[O]nce the mission is completed, one of the most important elements in the mission debrief is the discussion of "lessons learned." What are we going to take away from this operation to help us improve as a team and always develop as an organization? [25]

Another military veteran developed a training program called Afterburners, based on the steps fighter pilots take after each mission. In *The Debrief Imperative*[26] (FastPencil Premiere, 2011), by William Duke and James Murphy, the retired air force pilot Murphy explains:

> Debriefing is a specialized technique refined over millions of hours of flying and decades of trial and error in military aviation . . . it was developed by both the U.S. Navy and Air Force and is used after every military flight, bar none. It has saved countless lives, led to near-instantaneous improvements in systems, practices and plans, and is making the next generation of pilots better than the last. . . .
>
> As fighter pilots, we debriefed after *every* mission we flew. For instance, after a simulated air-to-air combat mission, we'd come home, take off our name tags, peel off our rank, get into a room and talk it over. Nothing held back. *How'd we do? Where did we go wrong? What did the adversaries throw at us that we hadn't planned for? Were the plans*

---

25. Brent Gleeson, "From the Battlefield to the Boardroom: A Navy SEAL's Guide to Leadership Success (Part 1 of 3)" *Forbes*, September 18, 2012, http://www.forbes.com/sites/brentgleeson/2012/09/18/from-the-battlefield-to-the-boardroom-a-navy-seals-guide-to-business-leadership-success-part-1-of-3/.0

26. *The Debrief Imperative*, William Duke and James Murphy (FastPencil Premiere, 2011), Foreward.

*clear?* The debrief helped us perform better as a group and perform better as individuals. [emphasis added]

If the process helps SEALs and fighter pilots, is there any reason to think others would not benefit from it? Conceptually the process seems like it should work. Experientially, it seems like it does. It is impossible to quantify how much better the SEALs and fighter pilots perform because of these debriefs, but these two testimonials are fairly compelling.

I suspect many lawyers believe they already do this assessment. Perhaps they do, but I suspect few do it with the rigor needed to extract all of the lessons available to be learned, fewer still implement changes in their practices as a result, and even fewer have involved their clients in the process.

Let me offer a real-life example. Two of my colleagues and I tried a case for DSW (world's greatest shoe store!). We prevailed on both the claim against DSW and DSW's counterclaim. It was home run result by any definition. A few weeks after the trial, my colleagues and I met and went through an after-action assessment. After a few minutes of feeling good and talking about all of the things we did well, we talked about things we could improve. The process was difficult because we don't like to admit imperfection. But after a while, we realized there were several things we could have done better and that while we hadn't paid a penalty in this case, it was foreseeable that under different circumstances we could. The more "opportunities for improvement" we identified, the better we felt because we knew our preparation for the next trial would be that much more complete. And because we shared our conclusions with others in the firm, they can now avoid making the same mistakes. Likewise, I have learned much from the shared experiences of colleagues who have gone through similar assessments.

This process is critical to creating a virtuous circle, which is shown in Figure 13.1.

**Figure 13.1**  Virtuous Circle

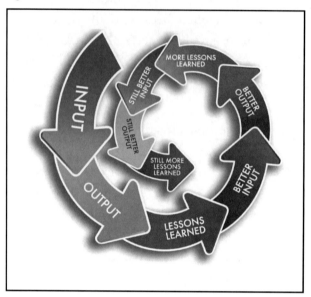

The continuous learning is critical to adjusting your pricing, improving your outcomes, and deepening relationships with your clients.

How does this fit in with value fees? If the goal is to maximize your profit when you quote a fixed fee (whether on a case or a portion of a case), you maximize your profit by reducing your cost of production. After-action assessments help decrease the cost of producing results because they help you get better at what you do.

Entire books have been written on how to conduct effective after-action assessments, and I highly recommend *The Debrief Imperative*, mentioned earlier in this chapter. One of the authors, James Murphy, recommends the STEALTH Debrief. In this case, STEALTH does not mean secrecy, but instead:

S—set the time (Debriefing should be part of the plan, project, or mission.)

T—tone (nameless and rankless)

E—execution vs. objectives (Review the execution and determine the results—the successes and errors.)

A—analyze execution (Seek root causes for each success and error.)

L—lessons learned (clear and precise)

T—transfer lessons learned (transmit and store)

H—high note (End with a positive summary.)

Murphy writes about each of these elements at a granular level, but the bottom line is that everyone on the team must be involved and feel no risk in offering criticism or asking questions. Lessons learned, both positive and negative, must be specific and actionable and must be shared with others who can benefit from them.

After-action assessments are so important that Peter Senge, in *The Fifth Discipline* (Doubleday, 2006), stated: "Many conclude that it borders on dereliction that their organizations invest so few resources in studying what has succeeded and failed in their past strategies. . . ."

It is imperative for the leader to set the right tone—"it isn't who's right, it's what's right." Self-criticism is an incredibly hard thing to embrace, but it is essential to creating high-performing teams. If the boss is never wrong, what is the point of the analysis? Everyone must embrace continuous improvement, and the leader must demonstrate the importance of that commitment.

If you go through this process, you will reduce the number of errors made in the future. You will find yourself doing various things better, faster, and, as result, at lower cost. You will find creative releases that help you develop better ways to do things, better ways to make yourself a better lawyer, and better ways to accomplish your clients' objectives.

An after-action assessment form is in the Appendix.

# Chapter 14
## THE CLIENT EXPERIENCE

During Bill Clinton's presidential campaign in 1992, one of his campaign strategists, James Carville, famously coined the phrase "It's the economy, stupid" to help bring focus to the campaign's theme. With a slight adjustment, the message to private practice lawyers is the same: "It's the client, stupid." No one matters more. At least no one *should* matter more. But lawyers too often find themselves putting their own interests ahead of their clients. Certainly that is so with hourly billing. But the issue needs to be looked at on a far grander scale.

When clients walk into your office, what do they see? Expensive furniture or something that suggests a focus on value? I recently entered a New York lawyer's office, and the client I was with said, "You know what I see when I walk in this building? High overhead. You know what I see when I walk in this office? High cost structure." Lawyers rarely look at the world through their clients' eyes, and as a result, many lawyers have strained relationships or even "just fine"[27] relationships with their clients. If that doesn't scare us,

---

27. People say "just fine" when they don't care enough to help the other person improve. How many times have you told a waiter the food was "fine" when you had already decided never to return to the restaurant?

nothing will. We need to develop powerful, positive relationships with our clients.

Tom Peters describes how this is done in the business world. Peters has been an in-demand business consultant and speaker since he and Robert H. Waterman Jr. wrote *In Search of Excellence* (Harper and Row, 1982) over thirty years ago. In his speaking, Peters highlights the evolution of "client service" and describes the movement as shown in Figure 14.1:

**Figure 14.1**   The Evolution of Client Service

| |
|---|
| Raw Materials |
| Goods |
| Services |
| Spellbinding Experiences |
| Dreams Come True |
| Lovemark |
| Customer Success/Game-Changing Solutions |

This is a value-added ladder—in reverse. A similar ladder has evolved in law. It is no longer acceptable to tell the client what the law is. It is no longer acceptable to simply be an advisor or a problem solver. As Tim Corcoran has written, "quality lawyering is merely table stakes. It is how outside counsel manage the relationship that matters most."[28] Managing a relationship is entirely about creating, preserving, and growing it, about making the client experience so special that clients can't imagine working with any other lawyer. Any other objective is setting the bar too low.

Here's why. If you are like most lawyers, others can do what you do. The challenge is to give clients an experience unlike any other, to

---

28. Timothy B. Corcoran, "The Changing Definition of Value," *Law Practice* Magazine 39, no. 6 (November/December 2013): 47.

provide service that makes them successful in an environment with demands greater than we have ever seen. If outside counsel are not aspiring to provide service in this fashion, they risk losing their clients to those who provide this premium service.

Think about it in this light. There are a sizable number of people who when they decide to buy a new laptop immediately head to the nearest Apple store and buy a MacBook. They happily pay several times more for their Apple product than they would pay for most PCs available at Best Buy or some other store. Why? Because of the Apple experience—everything from ease of use to staff at the Genius Bar who help configure computers and provide live in-person help rather than a PC call center in some part of the world.

As the seller of a service, do you want to sell to the Apple buyers (those relatively indifferent to price) or the PC buyers (those looking for a bargain)? There is nothing wrong with selling to PC buyers, but the difficulty experienced by companies like Dell and HP only illustrates the benefit of selling to those willing to pay a premium.

As the buyer of a service, do you want a service provider focused solely on cost, or do you prefer a provider who is focused on the quality and value of your entire experience? Are you willing to pay a bit extra if you feel you get more for your money? Of course you are! At least most of you are.[29]

It is plainly incumbent on lawyers to provide their clients with an extraordinary experience. But how? How do you do more than simply provide a lower price? Earlier chapters have covered a handful of tools that work well together to create value for law departments. Those tools are a great place to start.

If you want to improve relationships with your clients, there are many other things you might consider doing. Following is a list. It is

---

29. We live in a world where no generalization is entirely accurate. The lesson lawyers need to learn from this truism is that trying to be all things to all people is the surest way to be nothing to everyone.

in no particular order of importance and is not complete. It is a starting point. Every experience must be tailored to an individual client's wants and needs. Each of these ideas is based on learning clients' needs and understanding them. This is accomplished only by discussion—and outside counsel must ask questions.

1. Does the client have short-term budget issues? As year-end approaches, dollars can be tight, and a fee structure that defers payments until a new budget period may be useful.

2. When are budgets for the next year (fiscal or calendar) determined?

3. Is your fee charged to the law department or to a business unit? Does either create a particular sensitivity? (Experience suggests that business units hate surprises and uncertainty even more than most law departments.)

4. How active a member of the litigation team does your law department supervisor want to be? How can you maximize his or her contribution?

5. What are the factors on which your law department contact is evaluated?

6. What is the client's interest level in diversity? For a client committed to diversity, can you provide a simple pie chart showing what portion of the work tasks were primarily handled by each of your team members so the client knows diverse lawyers are being fully utilized on matters?

7. What are the biggest headaches your client has faced with other firms? What are the biggest headaches the client has experienced with *your* firm?

8. Does your client use Lean or Six Sigma in business? If so, has the law department used it as well? Is your contact keen on process improvements? How can you draw on his or her knowledge and experience?

9. What is your client's taste for disaggregation of services to drastically reduce litigation costs? Is the client willing to conduct beta tests to determine whether the savings third parties can provide can be achieved with the same or better work quality? What are you prepared to do to help achieve those benefits?

10. What opportunities exist to resolve your matter sooner (if that follows your client's objectives) so it is no longer a distraction?

11. Is your client interested in checklists so things like potential removal of a case or examining for indemnity rights are not overlooked?

12. Does your client's law department have budget goals? If so, do you have any ideas that would help the department achieve these goals?

13. Are there things your client could do differently to reduce the chance of being sued again on a matter like yours? Should the law department consider changes to the way it handles cases? For example, with so much of a case tied up in documents, should document review be accelerated?

14. Do you regularly ask the client how you and your firm could be better at what you do? At what you do for the client?

15. Has your client experimented with different staffing models, using a team of very senior lawyers on a fixed fee basis rather than the usual silo that ranges from junior associate up to most senior partner?

16. Does your client want to review all pleadings in a case or only certain types? How far in advance of filing does the client want to see the draft? Have you confirmed there are no scheduling issues so it is more convenient for the client to see the draft sooner on each particular filing?

17. Is there anything you can do to make your client's job easier? Provide case reports in advance of law department

meetings? Prepare some slides for a presentation about the case? Be there to help answer questions at a key meeting?

18. Have you visited your client face-to-face lately? Even with distant clients, face-to-face meetings a few times a year are valuable.

19. Have you asked your client for a "stretch goal"[30] for reducing litigation spend and thought of some ideas that would help the client do so?

20. Have you asked in January what you could do to make your contact look great by year-end?

Whatever the tool, whatever the discussion, each client has a set of expectations as to how the engagement should look and feel, and all clients have ideas about what makes life easier, what makes them look better, or, conversely, what types of issues create internal headaches. Extraordinary service is learning those things and providing what is valued and avoiding what is problematic or does not create value.

This sounds easier than it is. Few lawyers judge the value of their work through their clients' eyes. But no matter how good a job you think you do, if your client does not agree, you have failed to provide world-class service. This does not mean playing yes-man to your clients. They hate that. It means telling clients what you think and why, but recognizing that the decision on what to do and how to do it is ultimately theirs to make. Once that decision is made, you must execute with passion.

Those who raise objections to this concept do not understand their clients. Clients are sophisticated at judging the value of your

---

30. A stretch goal is sometimes referred to as a BHAG, or Big Hairy Audacious Goal. According to Wikipedia, a BHAG is a "strategic business statement . . . which is created to focus an organization on a single medium-long term organization-wide goal which is audacious, likely to be externally questionable, but not internally regarded as impossible." http://en.wikipedia.org/wiki/Big_Hairy_Audacious_Goal (accessed March 20, 2014).

performance, and they are doing so whether it is expressly acknowledged or not. They will simply not rehire you if they believe you provided poor value. More importantly, having an active, involved in-house lawyer on your team is a major asset. As an outside lawyer, no matter how many times you have represented the client, you will never know as much about the client and its people as the lawyer who represents them 24/7. In-house counsel bring critical knowledge to the team, and only a fool eschews it.

Recognizing these things, at Valorum we embraced the client's role as the judge of value. Every invoice we have ever sent, regardless of fee structure agreed upon, contains a Value Adjustment Line. The VAL contains this instruction: "Exceptional service and value are the standards we live by. If, for any reason, you do not believe that the services we provided should be valued as agreed, we encourage you to make any adjustment—up or down—that you believe is warranted." There is then a space for the value adjustment and a box for the new total due.

These things are a baseline. Outside the legal world, there has been a massive evolution in what is considered good customer service. You used to simply buy a hammer at Home Depot. Now when you go to Home Depot to buy a hammer, you get training in how to select the right hammer, courses in how to use it, personal advice on how not to misuse it, and so forth. Appliances are not only delivered but also installed and repaired. And so forth. The application to the service you provide to clients should be obvious. (And if it is not, good luck with that!)

In this book, alternative or, more precisely, value fees are a critical tool in providing great service. If your mindset is that alternative fees should be the same as the fees your firm would bill if you were handling the matter on an hourly basis, you are missing the boat entirely. The pressure on most matters is to lower the cost of securing the same or better output. If your fee is not accomplishing this important objective, you are failing your client.

# Chapter 15
## SOME THOUGHTS ON PRICING

Pricing is the cornerstone for effective alternative fee arrangements and is one of the most difficult tasks lawyers face. This is true whether you are committing to a fixed fee or preparing an honest budget for a client who intends to hold you to it. While experience is a great teacher, there are unknown variables, including your opponent and the court. Sometimes a price quote is required before you even know the identity of opposing counsel or in which court the matter will be filed or the name of judge who will handle the matter.

These are among the difficulties that drive lawyers back to safe environs—the hourly rate. If you don't know the identity of opposing counsel, just bill hourly. If the court is unknown, bill hourly. But the business world has taught us that unknowns must be addressed, and that lesson also applies to lawyers.

There are some important precepts that affect pricing, especially for smaller firms.

1. Not all dollars are of equal value. Guaranteed dollars are worth more than uncertain dollars. Guaranteed dollars allow firms to plan according to a known base. More certainty about revenue, at least for a base, allows for better planning and risk assessment. For example, if the rent and

payroll are covered, it is easier to justify a riskier investment on another matter.[31]

2. Dollars from repeat clients are also worth more than dollars from new clients or one-off clients because there are fewer marketing expenses associated with generating the revenue.

3. The goal is total profit, not profit on every hour. Every hour worked does not cost the firm the same amount, so there is no reason a client should pay the same for every hour. For firms, there is virtually no incremental cost when a lawyer works twenty additional hours in a month. Any cost the firm must consider, like a bonus for someone who continually works hard and produces more, can be considered in pricing.

4. Every hour does not produce the same value for the client. Hours are a firm-facing metric. Outputs are client facing.

The most-often-asked question about alternative fee arrangements is how to determine the amount of the fee. There are many answers to this question. But before we talk about pricing, it is important to talk about pricing philosophy.

Except in the rarest of circumstances, no single law firm is the only candidate for an engagement. That means there is a market, and a client will have priorities, such as total cost, quality, confidence, and predictability of cost. It is important for firms to keep these factors in mind and develop a pricing philosophy. **SPOILER ALERT!** The traditional philosophy of billing more hours does *not* work.

Every firm must have its own approach. Fred Bartlit of Bartlit Beck has described its pricing philosophy as determining what a top large firm would charge and then cutting that number substantially

---

31. This is true for smaller firms but probably not true at all for big firms, where one client's total fee may not be "material." As such, this is an example of how clients can often enter into far less expensive arrangements with smaller firms.

to a fixed monthly fee, with the difference going into a holdback bucket. Depending on the firm's performance, it can earn multiples of the holdback bucket.

Valorum's approach is different. For portfolios that extend over time, our goal is to increase profit by reducing cost, allowing us to lower prices in the future. Our concept is shown in Figure 15.1:

**Figure 15.1**   Valorum Pricing Philosophy

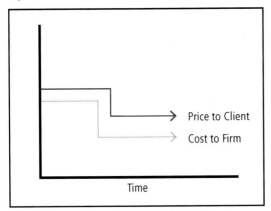

Price to Client

Cost to Firm

Time

Depending on the holdback or potential premium to the firm, we will agree to lower the price line.

If you are not comfortable with risk, do not use fixed fees. Figure 15.2 is one example of the way many people feel about fixed fees in litigation:

**Figure 15.2**   Opinion about Fixed Fees in Litigation

**Jason Gottlieb** @Jgottlaw
@Conduit_Law @LegalBusinessUK Do not fully agree. Cannot predict or control what opposing party does in #litigation matters. #morefees #law

This tweet expresses the sentiment, actually the fear, many lawyers cannot overcome when asked to fix their fee: uncertainty. What if [fill in the blank] happens? One lawyer recently wrote what many believe: "[T]he cost of litigation is never completely predictable."[32]

This is a misstatement. The time that must be spent on litigation may not be predictable (and I believe even that statement is inaccurate), but there is no reason the *cost* of litigation must be unpredictable simply because the time required cannot be predicted to the minute. Cost is unpredictable only because many lawyers insist it be tied to time.

There is no reason this has to be. Our clients confront unknowns and uncertainties every day. What do they do? *They deal with it.* I once sat on a panel with the general counsel of a company that tore down and rebuilt nuclear power plants on a turnkey, fixed price basis. When asked what he thought about the uncertainty of litigation as a reason for not fixing a price, he just laughed and said, "Welcome to the real world. Try dealing with the uncertainties of rebuilding nuclear power plants. If we can fix prices in that world, litigators can do it in theirs." Jeff Carr, the iconic general counsel of FMC Technologies, is equally direct: "We make and sell equipment on a fixed price basis that has to operate flawlessly on the ocean floor for more than twenty years. That's our world. I am unmoved that you can't figure out how long it will take to defend a lawsuit."

For so long, lawyers have seen themselves as immune from basic business concepts such as uncertainty of profit. This is just a variation on the "we're special" belief that hijacked the profession long ago. It's a sense of entitlement, pure and simple. Lawyers believe they are entitled to earn a profit on each hour they bill—there is a significant profit margin built into each lawyer's hourly rate. That is not the way of the business world, and more clients than ever are losing patience with the legal world's argument.

---

32. Ursula A. Taylor, "Managing the Cost of Litigation," *Corporate Counsel* (Butler, Rubin, Saltarelli & Boyd, July 2013), http://www.butlerrubin.com/wp-content/uploads/July-2013-OP-Article.pdf.

Fred Bartlit famously describes quoting AFAs as akin to drilling for oil. Sometimes you end up with a dry well. Never having drilled for oil, I can't comment, but the fact is that some fixed fees are better than others. Some contingency fee or reverse contingency fee agreements pay off handsomely. Others not so much. Welcome to the world of uncertainty. It may not be your cup of tea. But remember to think about how your clients feel about AFAs.

## TIME TO KNOWLEDGE—ROLE IN PRICING

The time between engagement and when lawyer and client have adequate information to make informed decisions is terribly important. Traditionally, knowledge is accumulated slowly. At the point where there are enough facts to make the best decisions, many hours have passed, and significant fees have been paid. The ability to accelerate time to knowledge allows for better earlier decision making, as shown in Figure 15.3. This can dramatically lower the cost of producing results.

**Figure 15.3**   Time-to-Knowledge Graph

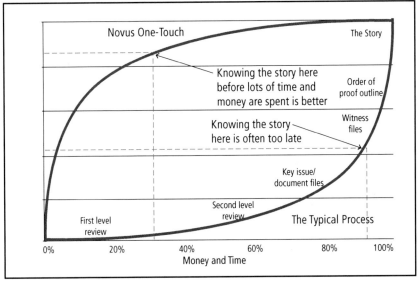

It is difficult to overstate the importance of the concept of time to knowledge in reducing costs. When concentrated, work is more efficient, and one major effect of the focus on time to knowledge is the efficiency with which knowledge is gained. On top of that, acquiring knowledge earlier leads to more targeted conduct throughout a lawsuit and enhances the ability of all involved to make better decisions sooner.

This is true whether the fee is data driven or created organically for a particular matter. The client's commitment to early knowledge is important to ascertain.

When a lawyer is engaged, the first question is whether there is data to be mined about the fees previously charged for similar cases. Data can come from firm history with handling similar cases or from how much the client has paid for similar cases. Data does not answer the question of price, but it provides important information that must be considered.

Consider the results of a search for past pricing. The data is likely to cluster in some fashion, as shown in Figure 15.4. When data doesn't cluster, it means that there is enough variation in the cases that one must be careful relying on the data. But generally data is informative.

**Figure 15.4**   Data Cluster

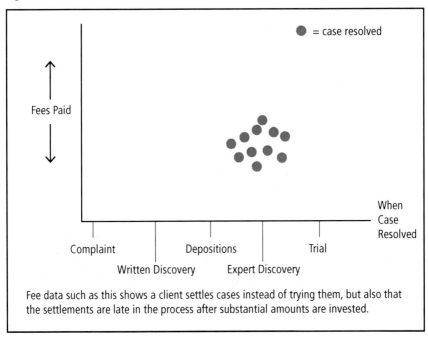

Fee data such as this shows a client settles cases instead of trying them, but also that the settlements are late in the process after substantial amounts are invested.

When one sees a data cluster, it gives confidence that the cluster is a reasonable point for pricing (see Figure 15.5).

**Figure 15.5**   Using Data Cluster for Pricing

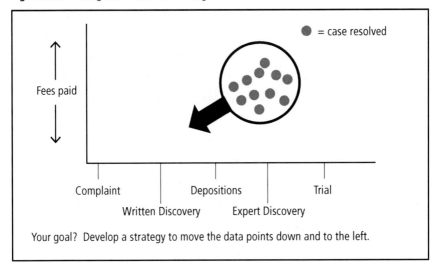

Your goal? Develop a strategy to move the data points down and to the left.

When clusters exist, clients want to use the clustered information to drive a lower price. So the firm's objective should be to lower the historic cluster price *and* reduce the time spent on matters. Those two factors are related. If you cannot accomplish a reduction in cost, you are simply giving clients what they already have, which they find unsatisfactory.

The reduction of cycle time allows firms to allocate their resources in a more focused manner, a key factor in lowering costs. The other task required is to mine the data to determine the basis for the historic costs. Were things done that did not need to be done? Could some tasks have been avoided? Was there work that could have been outsourced for better value? And so on. Data tells a story. Learn it.

It is common for cases to arise where neither client nor firm has data. For Valorem, since all of the partners came from other firms that were disinclined to share their historic data, we began with no data, so virtually all matters were priced organically. Sometimes clients have not collected data and are not prepared to make the investment to study it, or firms or clients have data where the number of data points is too small to be reliable.

There are a variety of methodologies used to create an organic price. One is a ground-up manner, identifying everything that is likely to happen and figuring out how much time it will take to do those things. This is akin to creating a budget, but it suffers from its reliance on hours and is little more than an hourly fee dressed up. A second method is the "gut feeling," where someone with experience says, "This kind of case should cost $XXX,XXX to litigate." The imprecision of this method is obvious, as is the lack of rigor in the process. At best it is a check on a price developed through some other approach. Both of these techniques derive their essence from past experience based on hourly work. Both ignore the risk to the client and the value lawyers bring to the matter.

Recognizing that time actually spent on a matter is not the driving force in setting a price, one must look to other factors. The following are the factors that influence the price:[33]

1. **Personnel involved.** Each person on a team has a cost. Knowing who is involved is critical.

2. **Time to trial.** This is a Parkinson's Law[34] issue. Work expands to fill the time that is available. We know cycle time is a significant contributor to cost.

3. **Expected stops and starts.** This is related to number 2. Will work be continuous or sporadic? Stopping and restarting takes extra time and effort.

4. **Case locale.** Is the forum a rule-intensive forum (e.g., California) where a great deal of time and attention is spent on fighting about rule compliance?

5. **Opposing counsel.** Are we dealing with lawyers we know, lawyers with a reputation, and so forth? Do we know their fee arrangement? It makes a difference as to their incentive to be efficient and reasonable.

6. **Case dimensions.** The number of parties and the complexity of the issues are important. More parties and greater complexity raise the cost.

7. **Importance to client.** The more attention a case commands at senior levels of the client company, the more attention it will command from your team.

8. **Relationship with client.** If you have an existing relationship with the client or have an opportunity for additional work, your costs for marketing and business development

---

33. In the appendix, I have included a spreadsheet that I use as part of my pricing efforts.
34. According to Wikipedia, "Parkinson's Law is the adage which states that 'work expands so as to fill the time available for its completion.'" http://en.wikipedia.org/wiki/Parkinson%27s_law (accessed March 20, 2014).

are reduced. If you are getting one-off matters, your marketing and business development costs will be higher.

9. **The work that will have to be done.** How many witnesses, documents, and issues?

10. **Capacity.** What is your capacity for additional work? If you take on the matter, do you have to hire new personnel or can your current personnel handle the workload? If you have capacity, your pencil can be very sharp.

11. **Business dynamics.** The motivation of the parties is very important. If the parties regularly do business together, the odds of an earlier settlement are higher.

12. **Prices being quoted by competitors.** You rarely know what others quote, but you should be trying to figure it out.

13. **Opportunities.** What doors are opened for you if you get the engagement? A high-profile matter or client may justify sharpening your pencil.

14. **Clarity of client objectives.** How clear and how reasonable are the client's objectives? If success is a moving target or objectives are conflicting, you cannot price as low as you otherwise might.

15. **Client attitude toward settlement.** If the client is unrealistic, it is likely the case will take longer to settle. The increase in expected time to settlement increases the fee.

16. **Client attitude toward disaggregation.** Will the client work with you to disaggregate work so that cost is lowered?

17. **Client risk tolerance.** Will the client make decisions based on significant but incomplete information or expect a high degree of certainty? The latter is more costly.

18. **Client personality.** Will the client be fun to work with or difficult? High-maintenance clients dramatically drive up the cost of handling a matter.

19. **E-discovery issues.** What e-discovery issues exist, and how equipped is the client to handle them? E-discovery has become a significant expense and is time-consuming.

20. **Lost opportunities.** What work will we not be able to perform if we take this engagement? If we have other irons in the fire, do we prefer those matters at the price under consideration, or do we prefer this matter because it is more certain?

21. **Cash flow analysis.** What is the certainty and length of cash flow from the matter if the price is accepted?

22. **Likelihood of recovering holdback.** What are our chances of succeeding on the merits and obtaining the holdback or a multiple of the holdback?

23. **Time commitment by team.** Knowing the team (see number 1), it is essential to determine how much time each person is spending on a matter.

The discussion about time is not intended to relate time commitment to the ultimate fee. But you do need to cover your costs. If lawyer A has a fully loaded cost of $35,000 per month and she is going to utilize half of her capacity on a matter for several months, the fee quoted needs to cover $17,500 per month. So the process is twofold: determining the cost and then the price. Cost is clearly influenced by time. But cost is fixed. It does not increase or decrease in a specific period if more or less time is spent. Consider this example: If a lawyer is writing a brief and spends 100 hours in a month doing so, the cost to the firm is the same as it would be if the lawyer spent 130 hours. The focus on cost and capacity become critical. Capacity can be fixed at whatever level a firm chooses, but, like any factory, the capacity number should reflect the ability to work at excess capacity at least for some period of time.

Creating a price involves identifying risks and how to share them. When you are pricing an entire case using a fixed fee, should the fee include trial? With so few cases going to trial, factoring in the cost of trial will inflate the price. How do you account for the chance of early settlement? From a client perspective, it makes no sense to agree to a price based on a case going to the point of trial if the thinking is that the case will settle early because of commercial expectations. A price that ignores the commercial expectations is likely to be too high for the client.

The weight accorded to each of the listed factors will vary from matter to matter and client to client. For some, there is no taste for pricing an entire case. The same variables can be used to price segments of cases, just as they can be used to price portfolios of cases.

## THINGS THAT ALWAYS SEEM TO COME UP

Some lawyers want to have their cake and eat it too. Many want protection against pricing error.

## Mulligans (Do-Overs)

In golf, a mulligan is a shot not counted against the score. A player who hits a poor shot simply pretends it didn't happen and hits another. And sometimes another. I have heard a number of lawyers pronounce that every fixed fee agreement should contain an out—a chance for the firm to declare a "do-over" if it does not feel the fee is as profitable as planned at the outset. I always have to ask whether these lawyers are kidding. Sadly, they are not. Just as sadly, the lawyers who want to include a mulligan never want to include one for the client. Apparently if a fee is working unexpectedly well for the firm, the client should just live with it.

Reciprocity issues aside, there are many reasons why mulligans should not be permitted on fixed fee agreements. First, the anticipation of an out makes the pricing process less important and less precise. You can take a chance on a fee agreement if you can have a do-over mid-stream. What incentive is there to be careful and precise in quoting the fee to start? Lowballing a fee quote to get business is an age-old trick that usually works only once ("Fool me once, shame on you. Fool me twice, shame on me"). It is certainly not a good practice.

Second, do-overs interfere with the client's budgeting. Enough said.

Third, do-overs interfere with trust. Alternative fee arrangements are built on trust.

The real issue hidden in the mulligan discussion is whether work is within scope. The easiest way to understand scope is to look at pricing from the standpoint of hiring a contractor to remodel your kitchen. If you decide midway through the project to have your bathroom remodeled as well, that work is outside the scope of the original quotation, and the contractor would provide a new price quote so you could decide whether to proceed. Likewise, if the original scope provides for laminate countertops and you later decide to upgrade to granite, the contractor will tell you exactly what the upgrade will cost so you can decide if you want to allocate your resources in that fashion. In the litigation context, work is scoped by issues, by events (a motion for summary judgment, for example), or for the case as a whole. But each period or set of services is based on a set of assumptions, and if those assumptions change, the lawyer and client will need to assess whether those changes should be reflected in the fee structure.

## Windfalls

Many times, in the final moments of agreeing to a fixed fee, lawyers are asked how to deal with the "problem of windfalls," which is the client's side of the mulligan issue. Prospective clients explain that if a case resolves early and we've been paid our fee, or the fee for that portion of the case, we will have received a windfall. By this, they mean that we will have been paid more than if we had been billing hourly. In many cases, this is classic have-your-cake-and-eat-it-too syndrome.

There are three reasons why the windfall issue is misplaced. First, it is based on the assumption that time is the proper measure of value, not outcome. For example, if a fee of $100,000 is considered fair for a $1 million outcome, it should not matter whether the outcome is obtained swiftly. Likewise, it shouldn't matter whether the lawyer had to put in far more effort than expected to achieve the outcome. It is the outcome that determines the value of the fee, not the time it takes to achieve the outcome.

There are two stories that illustrate the point, one I heard and one about which I have firsthand knowledge. The story I heard—it may be apocryphal—involved legendary lawyer Clark Clifford, who was asked to handle a delicate problem for a client. Clifford handled the problem to the client's delight and sent a bill for $50,000. The client called to complain, saying that Clifford had only spent a few hours on the matter. Clifford agreed to send a new bill with more details. The bill stated: "Calls to resolve matter—$1,000; knowing who to call to resolve matter—$49,000." The outcome, not the time, was the critical factor.

In the other story, a lawyer who had agreed to handle a matter for a fixed fee secured a dismissal without payment, based on a relationship she had developed with opposing counsel. When the client complained about the windfall, the lawyer offered to ask opposing counsel to reinstate the case so that discovery could be taken and then dismissal could be had on summary judgment. Facing that offer, the client realized the foolishness of the complaint. The focus must be on outcomes, not time to secure them.

The second reason the windfall concern is misplaced is that clients are generally unwilling to address the flip side, where firms invest far more time than anticipated. Clients that raise the windfall argument rarely raise the loss issue, and there are few stories of clients agreeing to pay more if a firm overworks a case. The real answer is that if clients feel that value is demonstrated by time, they should simply agree to pay an hourly rate.

Finally, we always tell our clients that we want to be paid based on the value we provide. To that end, if a case resolves early because the two CEOs worked something out right after we were engaged, we did not add value to the outcome and don't expect to be paid as if we did. That is why every bill we send has a Value Adjustment Line that allows the client to adjust the amount due so that *in the client's mind*, the amount paid equals the value the client believes we provided.

## What If . . . ?

No matter what fee structure is employed, it is possible to "what if" it beyond recognition. Even using hourly rates can involve lots of what-if questions. In the hourly model, the answer is always the same: Pay the lawyer for time spent. But the alternative fee ground is less trodden, so the answers are not always as obvious or known. This lack of predetermined answers is why everyone who has experience with alternative fees has learned how critical trust is to making the fees work.

Trust between lawyer and client has become a casualty of the hourly billing model, replaced by a general wariness. Virtually all clients carefully review legal bills, looking for mistakes (that invariably favor the law firm), excessive billing, and charges for work or expenses that were not approved. Some clients do this manually, some use electronic billing software, some have bills audited. Think about that—within the last decade or so, the entire profession of reviewing legal bills became necessary.

Invoices based on fixed fee arrangements do not need to be reviewed with this same jaundiced eye. It takes mere seconds to tell if the invoiced amount is the amount agreed upon. It is possible to rebuild trust. This trust becomes necessary when dealing with the what-if questions that occasionally arise. The times when an AFA goes off the rails are few. But they can happen. When they do, lawyer and client must discuss how to handle the situation. Both sides need to trust each other to be fair and reasonable. Clients have to trust that their lawyers are not going to be seeking increases to the fee simply because some unanticipated work is required. Such increases take away the predictability and certainty that clients value. On the other side, in rare circumstances where some unexpected event or development occurs, lawyers have to know that clients will be flexible in allowing upward changes to the fee. But clients also have a right to expect lawyers to lower the fee if developments after the fee agreement result in less work being required. Trust and fairness must run both ways.

# Chapter 16

*The defenders of the status quo are paid professional advocates. They are skilled and accomplished. And they will come up with arguments and what-ifs in a last-ditch effort to prevent change from occurring. The arguments are unavailing, like trying to stop a steamroller simply by standing in front of it as it moves down the road.*

Alternative fees can raise some simply addressed accounting issues.[35] The first issue is when a firm is allowed to recognize fees it receives under retainer agreements. For example, according to the Illinois Supreme Court,[36] there are three types of retainer agreements.

- **Classic retainer.** Funds paid by a client to secure a lawyer's availability for a specified period on a specified matter are considered a classic retainer. The money is earned by the lawyer immediately upon payment, and the client relinquishes all interest in its return. Classic retainers should not be deposited into a lawyer's client trust account.

- **Security retainer.** This is a payment for prospective services, and the client holds an interest in the funds until the services are actually rendered. It is the most common form of retainer.

---

35. I am not an accountant, and you should not rely on this chapter to deal with the issues. Seek accounting advice from your own professional advisor.
36. I have not attempted to conduct a fifty-state survey on the accounting issues potentially raised by using AFAs. Be sure to examine the rules in your own state.

The typical version is that the firm bills against the retainer and withdraws funds when an invoice is issued. Any unused portion of the retainer is returned to the client. Thus, security retainers remain the property of the client and *must* be deposited in a client trust account until the lawyer applies the money to charges for services actually rendered.

- **Advance payment retainer.** Funds paid to a lawyer under this retainer are intended by the client to be present payment in exchange for the commitment to provide legal services in the future. Ownership of this retainer passes to the lawyer immediately upon payment, and funds should not be deposited in the client trust account. An example of an advance payment retainer is where a debtor wants to have sufficient funds beyond the reach of a creditor to secure legal counsel. See *Dowling v. Chicago Options Associate, Inc.,* 226 Ill.2d 277 (IL 2007).

Funds that are held in a lawyer's client trust account cannot be recognized as revenue, meaning the firm cannot use those funds to pay its bills and the funds cannot be distributed as profits.

In Illinois and other states, fixed fees are not considered retainers and therefore can be recognized as revenue upon payment. The most important distinction is that there is no expectation that any portion of a fixed fee agreement will be refunded.

Fixed fees can present accounting issues for clients as well, generally in arrangements that involve holdbacks.[37] For example, in ordinary circumstances, when a client receives a bill for $100,000, the client is obligated to book the entire $100,000 as an expense. But what are the obligations if the parties have agreed that 20 percent of the bill is to be held back until the end of the engagement?

---

37. The assumption here is that many clients use the accrual method of accounting, and lawyers use cash-basis accounting.

For companies using cash-basis accounting, the answer is easy. They book the $80,000 obligation and only book the holdback if and when it is paid. But for companies using the accrual method, the answer is not so easy. The safe approach is to book the holdback amount as an expense at the time it is incurred. If circumstances eventually dictate that the entirety of the holdback is not paid, it can be reversed (if in the same year) or offset against the current year's expense.

Clients have their own accountants and accounting practices and will determine how they will meet any obligation to pay their lawyers. The issue should not be overlooked.

# Chapter 17
## ETHICAL CONSIDERATIONS

I have heard more than one lawyer suggest that nonhourly fee arrangements are unethical because Model Rule of Professional Conduct 1.5 requires a fee to be based on "the time and labor required," as if that phrase is the sum total of the Rule. Arguments against value billing are not surprising. Those threatened by these changes have naturally attempted to derail them, including, predictably, by suggesting these changes to established ways are not permitted under existing ethical rules governing the professional conduct of the lawyers.

The truth is that the ethical path for the nonhourly fees discussed in this book is as marked and visible as the path trodden for traditional work practices. The Rules of Professional Conduct are broad and flexible and are easily applied to the new value-based fees. By its nature, this discussion is a bit more "legal" than is my norm. For that, I apologize, but I believe it is important to arm every lawyer with ammunition on this topic.

Every fee arrangement, whether contingent, based on value or some other measure, or a more traditional hourly approach, must comply with ethical rules created by the states. Because most states follow the American Bar Association's Model Rules of Professional

Conduct (Model Rules or MPRC), those rules form the basis of our discussion.

## ETHICAL CONSIDERATIONS IN STRUCTURING VALUE-BASED FEES

The starting point for rules regarding fees is the Model Rule concerning fees. Model Rule 1.5 requires any agreement for fees and expenses to be reasonable under the circumstances and to be appropriately communicated to the client. MRPC 1.5(a) sets forth eight nonexhaustive factors to guide the assessment of a fee's reasonableness:

(1) the time and labor required, the novelty and difficulty of the questions involved, and the skill requisite to perform the legal service properly;

(2) the likelihood, if apparent to the client, that the acceptance of the particular employment will preclude other employment by the lawyer;

(3) the fee customarily charged in the locality for similar legal services;

(4) the amount involved and the results obtained;

(5) the time limitations imposed by the client or by the circumstances;

(6) the nature and length of the professional relationship with the client;

(7) the experience, reputation, and ability of the lawyer or lawyers performing the services; and

(8) whether the fee is fixed or contingent.

These criteria are necessarily broad and flexible. The factors that should be focused on vary according to the type of fee arrangement.

Many of the eight issues above (and possibly more) will and should be hashed out during the initial discussions with clients about the details of their matters and the scope of representation. Frank discussions with clients about the partnership and risk sharing are hallmarks of creating value-based fee arrangements. The Model Rules speak to this type of open communication between lawyers and clients when establishing a fee arrangement. Model Rule 1.5(b) requires that a lawyer communicate to the client the basis or rate of the fee and expenses, and the scope of the representation, in a timely manner and preferably in writing:

> The scope of the representation and the basis or rate of the fee and expenses for which the client will be responsible shall be communicated to the client, preferably in writing, before or within a reasonable time after commencing the representation, except when the lawyer will charge a regularly represented client on the same basis or rate. Any changes in the basis or rate of the fee or expenses shall also be communicated to the client.

This requirement is important where the lawyer and client have not developed an understanding concerning these issues because of prior representation. Comment 2 to Model Rule 1.5(b) describes the recommended manner of the communication under these circumstances:

> Generally, it is desirable to furnish the client with at least a simple memorandum or copy of the lawyer's customary fee arrangements that states the general nature of the legal services to be provided, the basis, rate or total amount of the fee and whether and to what extent the client will be responsible for any costs, expenses or disbursements in the course of the representation. A written statement concerning the terms of the engagement reduces the possibility of misunderstanding.

When communicating with clients about the structure of a fee arrangement, it is important to remember that the duties of competence and diligence require that, whatever the particulars of a fee arrangement, it should not unduly limit either the scope or the lawyer's loyal and zealous pursuit of the representation. A fee agreement should not be structured in a way that might create an undue risk that the lawyer will not devote adequate attention, expertise, and effort to a matter:

> A lawyer shall provide competent representation to a client. Competent representation requires the legal knowledge, skill, thoroughness and preparation reasonably necessary for the representation. [MRPC 1.1.]

> A lawyer shall act with reasonable diligence and promptness in representing a client. [MRPC 1.3.]

> Comment 5 to Model Rule 1.1 makes it clear that subject to these concerns, lawyers and clients are afforded substantial leeway to tailor their agreements to clients' business considerations:

The required attention and preparation are determined in part by what is at stake; major litigation and complex transactions ordinarily require more extensive treatment than matters of lesser complexity and consequence. An agreement between the lawyer and the client regarding the scope of the representation may limit the matters for which the lawyer is responsible. See Rule 1.2(c) [concerning scope of representation, discussed below].

Precisely because they are often creatively devised, tailored to individual business needs and client concerns, and depart from traditional practices, value-based fee arrangements sometimes give rise to ethical issues that are different from those that arise under billable hour fees. In all but the most unusual of cases, these issues are easily resolved or avoided altogether through effective lawyer-client communication (which is a good thing!) and careful drafting of the fee arrangement. Indeed, the same best practices that are instrumental in avoiding ethics issues in the billable hour context are instrumental to crafting value-based fee arrangements that better align the interests of lawyers and clients.

## VALUE-BASED FEES AND THE PHILOSOPHY OF THE ABA MODEL RULES

The ABA Model Rules provide substantial latitude for lawyers and clients to structure their fee agreements. Value-based fees fit comfortably within this space; in fact, the ABA Model Rules and value-based fees are in many respects mutually reinforcing. Even as the ABA Model Rules approve the methods employed by value-based fees, value-based fees further the goals of the ABA Model Rules.

> As the Restatement (Third) of the Law Governing Lawyers noted about one form of value-based fees: Contingent-fee arrangements perform three valuable functions. First, they enable persons who could not otherwise afford counsel to assert their rights, paying their lawyers only if the assertion succeeds. Second, contingent fees give lawyers an additional incentive to seek their clients' success and to encourage only those clients with claims having a substantial likelihood of succeeding. Third, such fees enable a client to share the risk of losing with a lawyer, who is usually better able to assess the risk and to bear it by undertaking similar arrangements in other cases. (*Id.* § 35, cmt. b.)

> Speaking of flat fees, the Court of Appeals for the District of Columbia said:

For the client, *[a flat fee]* "eliminate[s] the uncertainty, anxiety and surprise often found with hourly rates, especially in protracted litigation. . . ." *[Citation omitted]* For the lawyer, it "reward[s] efficiency and enable[s] the attorney to concentrate on the representation instead of fighting with the client over monthly bills[, and] provide[s] certainty of payment. . . ." *[Citation omitted]* (*In re Mance*, 980 A.2d 1196, 1204 (D.C. Ct. App. 2009) Note: Brackets in the original; italic brackets from author.

Thus, value-based fees are designed to better align the interests of lawyers and clients by shifting some of the risks involved in the representation onto the party with the most control over those risks—the lawyer. Both flat fee and performance-based fee arrangements encourage lawyers to resolve matters as quickly and efficiently as possible. Under hourly billing arrangements, in contrast, the risks of the representation rest primarily on the client. Lawyers and law firms have minimal risk exposure because they charge for the time worked regardless of their efficiency or the outcome. Hourly billing arrangements tend to result in needless tasks being performed in the name of thoroughness, disregarding the client's real interest in the work. Not to be overlooked is the conflict between lawyers and clients that frequently arises as clients police invoices to ensure they are not being overbilled.

The Model Rules in turn facilitate the efforts of lawyers and clients to devise and carry out value-based fee arrangements. The Rules forbid the most egregious abuses and also help identify and resolve some of the potential problems encountered by lawyers and clients in crafting value-based fees. Finally, lawyers are bound by the Rules to honor certain duties and obligations that require them to serve their clients' interests even when their personal or economic interests might dictate otherwise. The spirit of the Rules can, in many cases, fill the inevitable gaps in the terms of a value-based fee agreement.

## ENSURING REASONABLE FEES

One characteristic of many value-based fee arrangements is a limitation on lawyer fees and costs. While a fee based on billable hours might list the hourly rates charged by the lawyers who will work on a matter, this usually does not provide the client with much certainty as to the ultimate cost of the representation. The amount of work done will vary according to the vagaries of the case, the work habits of the lawyers, and many other factors over which the client has little knowledge or control. In contrast, value-based fees are often set at a fixed rate at the outset of the representation or set on some performance-related benchmark.

Model Rule 1.5, which requires fees to be reasonable under the circumstances, acknowledges the validity of these cost-saving efforts. Comment 5 to the Rule states that "it is proper to define the extent of services in light of the client's ability to pay." As the Comment makes clear, "the client's ability to a pay" raises ethical issues under hourly fee arrangements as well as value-based fees, and it warns that a lawyer "should not exploit a fee arrangement based primarily on hourly charges by using wasteful procedures."

In seeking to eliminate wasteful or unnecessary procedures, Rule 1.5 likewise stops lawyers from going too far in the other direction. Thus, Comment 5 says that an agreement "may not be made whose terms might induce the lawyer improperly to curtail services for the client or perform them in a way contrary to the client's interest."

But aside from prohibiting abusive practices, Comment 5 makes clear that communication is key. In attempting to address a client's desires to limit or control costs, a lawyer must anticipate and communicate to the client the "foreseeable" pitfalls and risks. As long as the client is advised of and consents to the risks, the limitations entailed by the fee do not pose an ethical issue.

It should be noted that what is a "reasonable fee" for the purposes of professional ethics, as considered above, may not be a reasonable fee for the purposes of a federal fee-shifting statute.[38] The Supreme Court's recent decision in *Perdue v. Kenny* is instructive in this regard (595 U.S. 542 [2010]). The Court reaffirmed that the lodestar method, in which the number of hours worked is multiplied by the prevailing hourly rates, "has, as its name suggests, become the guiding light of our fee-shifting jurisprudence." (*Id.* at 551; internal quotation marks omitted.) Accordingly, the Court has imposed stringent restrictions on the awarding of the sorts of performance-based enhancements that characterize many value-based fees—"we have repeatedly said that enhancements may be awarded in 'rare' and 'exceptional' circumstances"—and even then only after a burdensome and exacting showing by the party seeking the enhancement. (*Id.* at 552.) As the Court observed, "[W]e have never sustained an enhancement of the lodestar amount for performance. . . ." (*Id.*)

*Perdue* does not call into question, or even cast the slightest cloud over, value-based fee arrangements as a matter of professional ethics or contract law; it merely reaffirms that, as a matter of statutory construction, the Court does not interpret the term "reasonable attorney's fee" in certain federal fee-shifting statutes to include certain value-based enhancements, except upon an extraordinary showing.

The Eighth Circuit Court of Appeals recently clarified that the Supreme Court's opinion in *Perdue* does not implicate fee arrangements created at the outset of a representation. In *Little Rock School Dist. v. Arkansas*, the Eighth Circuit granted a motion for attorneys' fees under 42 U.S.C. § 1988 and 28 U.SC. § 1920 where the appellants' lawyers brought the appeal at reduced hourly rates but sought an award of attorneys' fees at their higher and normal hourly rate (674 F.3d 990, 996 [8th Cir. 2012]). The Eighth Circuit held that the Court in *Perdue* made clear that the enhancements to the

---

38. This may well also apply to any state-law counterparts, but I have not endeavored to make that analysis.

lodestar rate disallowed in *Perdue* were distinguishable from "rates initially set in a fee arrangement." (*Id.*)

Even though *Perdue's* relevance to value-based fee arrangements may be limited, the Court's reasoning in *Perdue* can be significant when discussing fee arrangements at the outset of a representation. Lawyers and clients should keep in mind the prevalence of the lodestar method when negotiating fee arrangements for matters that might involve an award of fees to the lawyer, whether under a federal fee-shifting statute or other statutes or contractual provisions. In the case of certain federal fee-shifting provisions, *Perdue* reminds us, it is only in the most exceptional cases that courts will be justified in awarding an enhancement for factors not already covered by the lodestar method, such as superior results or lawyer skill. Put differently, either the client must pay any performance-based bonus or the bonus will not be paid; the parties should not expect the court to enforce a value-based fee arrangement in an award of statutory fees.

Even when a party's right to fees is not based on a federal fee-shifting statute, a court may be reluctant to award a value-based fee and may instead resort to the more familiar lodestar method. As the Court pointed out in *Perdue*, the lodestar method furthers many of the public policy purposes animating fee-shifting statutes, which have little if any relevance to private fee arrangements.

In cases where courts may be asked to award fees,[39] lawyers should discuss the timekeeping issue with their clients. There is a cost to timekeeping, after all, but the risk of not being able to recover a fee because time records are not kept is never one that should be made without the client's consent. I believe it unlikely that clients will seek to impose this requirement in the absence of a realistic opportunity to recover fees.

---

39. It is a decidedly rare circumstance when courts award fees to begin, and even rarer when the possibility of such awards is not known at the outset of the case.

## PERFORMANCE-BASED FEES IN THE CIVIL CONTEXT

As an older version of the New York[40] ethics rules stated, "[c]ontingent fee arrangements in civil cases have long been commonly accepted in the United States in proceedings to enforce claims." (N.Y. City Assn. Bar Comm. Prof. Jud. Ethics Op. 1993-2, 1993 WL 765495, at *1[Dec. 15, 1993] [quoting EC 2-20 of the New York Disciplinary Rules].) Model Rule 1.5(c) expressly allows such fees: "A fee may be contingent on the outcome of the matter for which the service is rendered, except [in domestic relations matters and the representation of defendants in criminal cases]." State ethics rules approve of contingency fees in a wide range of contexts.

Noting the growing use of contingency fees outside the traditional context of personal injury cases, the ABA Standing Committee on Ethics and Professional Responsibility noted:

The use of contingent fees in these areas, for plaintiffs and defendants, impecunious and affluent alike, reflects the desire of clients to tie a lawyer's compensation to her performance and to give the lawyer incentives to improve returns to the client. The trend also may reflect a growing dissatisfaction with hourly rate billing. (ABA Comm. on Ethics and Prof. Responsibility, Formal Op. 94-389, at 2 [Dec. 5, 1994].)

Contingency and other performance-based fee arrangements raise several unique considerations.

- **Reasonableness.** As Comment 3 to MRPC 1.5 notes: "Contingent fees, like any other fees, are subject to the reasonableness standard of paragraph (a) of this Rule." Thus, a lawyer must determine the reasonability of a performance-based fee under the circumstances as well as the reasonability of the terms of the fee contemplated by the lawyer and client.

---

40. It is essential to remember that each state's ethical rules and opinions may differ; analysis and research must be done in a state-specific context.

- **Reasonable use of contingency fees.** In addition to certain domestic relations and criminal defense matters, a performance-based fee may be less appropriate in a routine matter where the outcome, especially the amount to be recovered, is relatively certain. In these circumstances, a lawyer's efforts add little to the amount a client recovers. However, even in these matters a contingency fee may be reasonable if the relative lack of risk is reflected in a smaller fee percentage. (See ABA Comm. on Ethics and Prof. Responsibility, Formal Op. 94-389 [1994].)

- **Reasonable contingency fees.** As the Restatement (Third) of the Law Governing Lawyers notes, contingency fees may present several anomalies. A contingency fee may be greater than the hourly rate fee of the same lawyer for the matter, because a "contingent-fee lawyer bears the risk of receiving no pay if the client loses and is entitled to compensation for bearing that risk." (*Id.* at § 35, cmt. c.) "Nor is a contingent fee necessarily unreasonable because the lawyer devoted relatively little time to a representation, for the customary terms of such arrangements commit the lawyer to provide necessary effort without extra pay if a relatively large expenditure of the lawyer's time were entailed." (*Id.*) However, such large fees become less reasonable to the extent that such effort or a significant period of risk is absent. Similarly, if a fee combines an hourly rate with a contingency, both the hourly rate and percentage will likely be lower than their corresponding amounts under a pure hourly billing or a pure contingency fee. (N.Y. St. Bar. Assn. Comm. Prof. Ethics NY Op. 697, 1997 WL 1068501, at *1 [Dec. 30, 1997].) Finally, the governing law may also impose a ceiling on the allowable percentage for a contingency fee or set other conditions, such as requiring a lawyer to offer the client an alternative basis for the fee.

## ETHICAL CONSIDERATIONS IN THE EARNING OF A FLAT FEE

A flat fee for an entire representation, or a phase or phases of a representation, is a component of many value-based fee arrangements. While flat fees are perfectly permissible under the ethical rules, how a lawyer maintains the flat fee and when a lawyer may treat that fee as "earned" raise some ethical considerations. At the outset of a flat fee engagement, the lawyer and client should fully understand and agree to the circumstances under which the lawyer's fees are deemed "earned" to ensure compliance with Model Rule 1.15.

Two provisions of this Rule are relevant. Model Rule 1.15(c) requires that a lawyer "shall deposit into a client trust account legal fees and expenses that have been paid in advance, to be withdrawn by the lawyer only as fees are earned or expenses incurred." Model Rule 1.15(a) forbids lawyers from commingling their own money with client funds. Together, these rules require a lawyer to segregate in a trust account or escrow any unearned portions of a flat fee paid by the client and to transfer any earned funds out of that account.

Complying with these requirements thus raises the question of when a flat fee is "earned." The emerging consensus holds that a flat fee is not simply earned upon receipt, irrespective of what the fee agreement might say. It must be deposited in a trust account until earned. A recent ethics opinion, District of Columbia Bar Legal Ethics Comm., Op. 355 (June 2010), summarizes the prevalent thinking on the issue as follows:

- Absent a contrary agreement, a lawyer must deposit a flat or fixed fee paid in advance of legal services in the lawyer's trust account. Such funds must remain in the lawyer's trust account until earned.

- The lawyer and client may agree concerning how and when the lawyer is deemed to have earned some, or all, of the flat fee. Such an agreement must bear a reasonable relationship to the anticipated course of the representation and must avoid excessive "front-loading."

- A lawyer and client could agree on withdrawals based on the application of an hourly rate to the lawyer's efforts. Withdrawals could be tied to events in a representation, such as completion of discovery, hearings, or the setting of a trial date, or to the completion of specific tasks, such as witness interviews, filing of motions, or, in a nonlitigation matter, the completion of specified draft documents. The lawyer and client can agree upon alternative milestones to address uncertainties about the future course of a representation. The lawyer and client can decide to divide a flat fee into monthly installments with an agreement that the monthly payment is earned at a specified point of the month.

- The agreement can also contain language reflecting that the lawyer will earn the entire fee at the conclusion of a representation even if certain specified milestones have never been reached.

- A written agreement or a writing evidencing the agreement is strongly recommended but not mandatory.

- Alternatively, a lawyer may place unearned funds in an operating account with informed consent from the client. To obtain such consent, the lawyer must explain to the client that the funds may also be kept in a trust account until earned and that placement in an operating account does not affect the lawyer's obligation to refund unearned funds if the client terminates the representation. The lawyer should also explain the additional protection offered by a trust account. For the lawyer's and client's protection, these disclosures should be in writing, even though the Model Rules do not mandate it.

Several courts have held that "an attorney earns fees only by conferring a benefit on or performing a legal service for the client." (*In re Mance*, 980 A.2d 1196, 1202 [D.C. Ct. App. 2009], *quoting, In re Sather*, 3 P.2d 403, 410 [Col. 2000] [en banc].) The D.C. Circuit Court of Appeals made clear that clients can agree to different arrangements for the disbursal of a flat fee as long as the clients are adequately informed of their rights and give informed consent as detailed above. (See *Mance*, 980 A.2d at 1206.)

Thus, there should be no concern that clients and lawyers have the freedom to craft a flat fee arrangement that governs when the lawyer "earns" a flat fee, as long as lawyers and clients have frank and detailed communication about what events trigger the earning of the flat fee. Such communication is essential anyway when crafting any type of value-based fee arrangements and is the diving board for the effective partnerships created by value-based fee arrangements.

# Chapter 18
## CLIENTS: BE BETTER BUYERS

**(Hint to Outside Lawyers: Know What Your Clients Want)**

Some in-house lawyers believe alternative fee arrangements are, conceptually at least, the preferred approach. They want to experience the benefits of alternative fee arrangements but do not know how to secure the benefits. Frequently these in-house lawyers ask their firms to propose an AFA. Many times this request is met with passive-aggressive behavior.[41] Firms promise to "get to it" but then never really do. Sometimes, indeed many times, when firms do respond, they do their Shakespearean best, showing their mastery of Act 2, Scene 2 of *Romeo and Juliet*, in which Juliet utters, "What's in a name? That which we call a rose by any other name would smell as sweet."

Firms often develop a proposal for a fixed fee that is the equivalent of the amount the client would expect to pay if the firm was billing hourly *and* the matter made it all the way to trial. Firms surprisingly are not shy about disclosing this pricing philosophy. The

---

41. According to Wikipedia, "Passive-aggressive behavior is the indirect expression of hostility, such as through procrastination, sarcasm, hostile jokes, stubbornness, resentment, sullenness, or deliberate or repeated failure to accomplish requested tasks for which one is (often explicitly) responsible." http://en.wikipedia.org/wiki/Passive_aggressive (accessed March 22, 2014).

managing partner of one Am Law 50 firm indicated at a corporate counsel conference that the benchmark for approving an AFA proposal was how it compared with what the firm would make if it billed hourly *and* the timing of the receipt of money. In other words, this managing partner would reject alternative fee proposals that delayed revenue even if the delay ultimately meant the firm would receive more revenue. He acknowledged that he needed the money to keep his profits-per-partner number where it needed to be.

Other managing partners have said they calculate fixed fee proposals by determining what the firm would bill by the hour, and some have said they use this approach to create a preliminary number and then add a risk premium to come up with their final proposal.

It is true that fees calculated in this fashion provide financial certainty to the client. The problem for the client is that proposals like these transfer all of the firm's potential risk of a lower fee (for instance, if the matter settles early) to the client. Conversely, the one potential benefit the client enjoys under an hourly model—turning off the meter if the matter settles early (as an example)—is taken away under these proposals. The upside of these agreements inures entirely to the firm. So the only thing alternative about the fee proposed is that it is certain. But because the certainty is equal to the maximum amount the client *might* have to pay, there is nothing positive for the client. Obviously not every firm calculates its AFA proposals by basing the AFA on some derivation of an hourly fee total. But enough do so that clients are advised to guard against it and to not assume that firms quoting AFAs have eschewed any connection to hourly billing. Here are suggestions for questions that will disclose how firms have determined their AFA proposals and whether they have made the client-focused changes needed for AFAs to work to the client's ultimate benefit.

## How did you determine your alternative fee? What metrics did you examine? What factors did you consider? What experience did you draw on? May I see your worksheet?

If a lawyer mentions hours in answering any of these questions, the lawyer probably has provided only a surrogate hourly rate number. But it is locked in. Early settlement? Client loses. Case goes the distance? Law firm covered. That is not risk sharing under any definition. Prices are set based on data or on the cost of personnel to the law firm.

If data exists, the goal is to reduce historic cost, and the data should provide insights into changes that can be made. For example, a different approach to experts or a different manner of handling document production and review are two of many ways to lower historic costs. The important thing is to study the data so a plan can be developed.

Absent data, several things go into pricing, as discussed in Chapter 15. The key insight for clients is whether a firm is using its costs in calculating price. For example, whether an associate spends twenty hours or forty hours on a project in the same pay period, the cost to the firm is the same even though the cost to the client is double. This understanding should be reflected somewhere in the firm's analysis.

## How do you handle cases differently under the alternative fee you quoted than you would if you were billing by the hour?

Everyone knows by now that those who are serious about alternative fees have learned to handle things differently, so the goal of this question is to find out how the firm has changed to better provide meaningful AFAs to its clients. Legal project management. Lean Six Sigma. Process mapping. These concepts mean something to people truly committed to alternatives because they are among the things that drive the cost of production down (and hence increase profit margins). But if firms are serious about reducing the cost of producing outcomes so they can maintain a strong profit margin even when lowering the cost to their clients, they will have some program, by whatever name, focused on reducing the cost of handling litigation. A firm that cannot provide chapter and verse on how it is driving down the cost of production is just a pretender.

If the answer is "We don't handle AFA matters differently," the client needs to ask, "How are you doing things differently now than you were three years ago? Be specific." The question should elicit some specific response—changed staffing, greater risk taking, more partner involvement at the front end—something to show procedures have changed significantly. And one would reasonably expect that the project and process tools just mentioned would be part of the law firm's culture, training, or application.

Finally, the most telling answer may well be that the firm handles AFA matters differently. If so, one must wonder why a new manner of handling AFA litigation is not good enough to use on hourly matters. Presumably, the answer indicates that a firm's AFAs are not the same as they used to be. But if the changes to improve the firm's efficiency and reduce the cost of handling the matter at hand have not been implemented on all matters, one must wonder why. There is no acceptable explanation of why a firm would not handle hourly matters as efficiently as it does nonhourly matters.

## What is your disaggregation strategy, and why do you use that strategy?

If there is no disaggregation strategy, the firm hasn't eliminated the fat. It's just that simple. For cases with a sufficient number of documents, the best answer, in my view, is that document review (not just first-level review, but all review right up until partners lay hands on the documents) should be outsourced. There are professional reviewers who do more, offering higher quality and more useful work product, than any law firm could consider, for a fraction of the cost. The cost difference is quantifiable and is money in the client's pocket. We are also close to a point where computerized review is an acceptable alternative and is likely less expensive than law firm review. Such alternatives must constantly be evaluated given the pace of change in the field.

## How did the firm change its hourly rate DNA?

Firms that operated for decades on an hourly rate model cannot flip a switch to become AFA firms. Learning how a firm identified what it needed to change, what it did to change, and what it still must change provides great insight. Does the firm have hourly targets? Does it provide bonuses based on hours billed? If either is true, the firm is still creating an incentive for associates to maximize their hours rather than to work efficiently. Are partners compensated based on revenue collected or profitability of their work? Are they penalized for any deficit to collection of 100 percent or rack rates? These pressures on partners impede effective deployment of AFAs.

A hidden part of firms' DNA is work product quality. Most firms only advance "the best" to partnership. Associates have learned to edit and reedit, to research every possible question a partner might ask or look at every case that could conceivably be relevant to a brief. If a firm does not recognize the value of efficiency, including understanding that there is a place for "good enough," it has yet to modify its DNA to operate effectively in an AFA world.

Few firms have eliminated these core features of operating under the hourly model. Failure to eliminate these features prevents firms from meaningfully lowering their cost of producing outcomes, which means there will be pressure to "get more" from clients because profit comes from adding top-line revenue rather than from lowering production costs and improving the profit margin. Until firms make these fundamental changes, they will never be able to deliver the value that can be found in true AFAs.

Lawyers are smart and effective advocates. Clients who fail to ask specific questions risk getting sold an inflated offering. Intelligent questions will expose the pretenders. And firms need to know how to truthfully answer these questions to show real change in their nature and character and their full embrace of value billing and value relationships.

# Chapter 19
## THE 50 PERCENT CHALLENGE

*"With a few notable exceptions, major law firms are not going to try to reinvent their profit model (assuming they have the wisdom to know how) to help clients cut costs 50 percent while allowing the law firm to continue generating revenues as it has done in the past."*

—Ken Grady, former general counsel, Wolverine World Wide Inc.

A while back, I heard from someone that noted legal futurist and scholar Richard Susskind[42] had predicted that companies would be reducing their legal spend by 50 percent over the next several years. It seemed like that kind of prediction would have garnered substantial press, so I e-mailed Susskind. He was kind enough to share that many general counsel were telling him that over the next three to five years they expected to reduce their legal spend by 30 to 50 percent. When I mentioned this prediction to other lawyers, the

---

42. Susskind is the author of, among other books, *The End of Lawyers?: Rethinking the Nature of Legal Services* and *Tomorrow's Lawyers: An Introduction to Your Future.* In the latter work, Susskind explains why law firms, legal institutions, and the legal profession are likely to change more radically over the next twenty years than they have over the past two hundred years. He serves as independent advisor to professional firms and to national governments.

immediate reaction was to debate higher percentage. Doing so misses the point. If he's off by 50 percent, law departments are still facing a 25 percent reduction in legal spend. Most of the reduction is likely to come from the ranks of outside counsel, since most law departments are operating leanly. Under any standard, the reduction is likely to be material.

While there is no way to determine whether Professor Susskind's sense of the market is correct, he has been so extraordinarily accurate with his predictions over the span of decades that only fools ignore his insights. We certainly know that his prediction is consistent with the "more for less" pressures that in-house lawyers face every day. So even if we focus on the low end of the range, 30 percent, the profession would still face major upheaval. No single tool or fee structure will generate those kinds of savings, though value fees, created by committed lawyers and combined with intelligent use of non-law-firm service providers, can come close.

There do not seem to be any indicia of change-focused DNA taking hold at major law firms. It is not surprising—successful firms are going to be the last to change. This phenomenon is true in every industry. One need only reflect on the auto industry to see the point. The Big Three became fat and happy while newer, more nimble firms from Japan created ways of producing high-quality vehicles at lower cost. By the time the Big Three figured out what was happening, their path toward bankruptcy (in the case of GM and Chrysler) was fixed.

Change at law firms is even more difficult because they are a collection of silos. If a partner doesn't like what the firm is doing, the partner takes his or her book of business and leaves. Why should that partner commit to new methods of work, pricing, and staffing if clients aren't demanding them? This happens with such frequency that the "churn" among partners is daily fodder in the legal media.

With it so easy for partners to pick up and leave, how can a firm galvanize the commitment needed to make any kind of real change?

Change at the periphery will not get any firm to the point where it can help a client cut expenses by 30 percent, let alone 50 percent.

So what is the answer for clients? If Ken Grady and so many others are right that most larger firms will not make the necessary changes, how do clients achieve the 30 to 50 percent cost reduction?

Write this down: *Solutions must be engineered.*

Solutions do not just magically occur. They rarely are the product of chance. Serendipity has proven itself a poor business strategy. The "more with less" problem requires a solution that is planned, analyzed, and executed. While the end does not require slavish adherence to a predetermined course, successful problem solvers begin with a vision of what the end should look like. They then engineer toward that vision.

Most of us embrace this concept in everyday life. For example, when we are traveling by car to an unfamiliar place, we use a mapping feature to instruct us how to get to the location.

We don't have to take a trip the way Lewis and Clark did, by venturing into the unknown with a hazy vision of the final destination. There are many tools we can use to figure out exactly where we are going and how best to get there.

The concept of working toward a vision is featured by Stephen Covey in his acclaimed book *The 7 Habits of Highly Effective People.* (Free Press, 1989) Habit 2 is "Begin with the end in mind." Author Ronald J. Baker gives an example in his book *Pricing on Purpose: Creating and Capturing Value* (Wiley, 2006):

> The application of this concept to pricing leads us to price-led costing. . . . Here is a great story, not a legal one, but a great one nonetheless: US soldiers stationed in Europe during World War II were attracted to the sporty British MG car. After the war, General Motors took a calculated risk designing and then manufacturing the Chevrolet Corvette, introduced in 1953, utilizing the

DuPont return on investment (ROI) formula to derive a price of $3,490.

As the Corvette was experiencing success, a competing automobile company took note—particularly one executive looking for his next big hit. When Lee Iacocca developed the Ford Mustang, he chose to reverse the order of car-making pricing. Rather than giving his engineers carte blanche to develop a sports car and then marking up the resulting costs to arrive at a price—as GM did—he solicited the opinions of potential customers as to what features they would want in a sports car and what price they thought they would be willing to pay.

Knowing people liked the Corvette, but thought it was too expensive at $3,490, Iacocca wanted the price to be low enough to entice the potential sports car enthusiast. He then went to his engineers and asked if they could manufacture a sports car with the desired features, and sell it for a price of no more than $2,500, while still turning an acceptable profit.[43]

Car buffs know the outcome—the engineers used the chassis from the Ford Falcon and met Iacocca's challenge on the price. How about the profits?

In the first two years, [the Mustang] generated net profits of $1.1 billion (in 1964 dollars), far in excess of what GM had made on the Corvette.[44]

Law firms engage in cost-plus pricing, which is the very antithesis of price-led costing. According to renowned business scholar Peter

---

43. Professional Pricing Society, "Price-Led Costing: The Wave of the Future," *The Pricing Advisor* (March 2007). Excerpt from *Pricing on Purpose: Creating and Capturing Value* by Ronald J. Baker (Wiley, 2006).

44. Ronald J. Baker, *Pricing on Purpose: Creating and Capturing Value* (Hoboken, NJ: Wiley, 2006).

Drucker: "Traditionally, Western companies have started with costs, put a desired profit margin on top, and arrived at a price. They practiced cost-led pricing."[45] This is precisely how law firms price their services. But the business world changed to price-led costing, described this way by Drucker: "[Price-led costing is where] the price the customer is willing to pay determines allowable costs. . . . Now, price-led costing is becoming the rule."[46]

Cost-driven pricing is one of Drucker's "five deadly sins" of business. Consumers do not see it as their job to ensure a profit for a manufacturer of products they buy. They care about price and quality. The manufacturer needs to figure out how to turn a profit within the price the customers are willing to pay. But law firm clients have refused to exercise their inherent power in this area and instead have enabled firms to continue to pursue cost-led pricing and steal them blind. The choice for law departments, shown in Figure 19.1, is a stark one:

**Figure 19.1**    Old Normal vs. New Normal

# Old Normal: Cost-Plus Pricing

Product ⟶ Cost ⟶ Price ⟶ Customers

# New Normal: Price-Led Costing

Customers ⟶ Value ⟶ Price ⟶ Cost ⟶ Product

For many law departments, the days of the old normal may be ending. Drucker states: "Starting out with price and then whittling down costs is more work initially. But in the end it is much less work than to start out wrong and then spend loss-making years bringing costs into line."[47] At least some clients now realize their inherent

---

45. Peter F. Drucker, *The Essential Drucker* (New York: HarperBusiness, 2012), 102.

46. Id.

47. Peter Drucker, "Management: The Five Deadly Sins," *The Independent*, November 3, 1993, http://www.independent.co.uk/news/business/management-the-five-deadly-sins-1501842.html.

power in the pricing area and are acting much more like consumers in demanding price-led costing to better align the value of a particular matter with the law firm's approach to it and the manner in which it is handled.

I am frequently asked for an illustration. I discussed Novus Law's innovative approach to document review in Chapter 12. There is now empirical data demonstrating that Novus can generate savings of 15 to 30 percent on the cost of litigation.[48] According to Novus CEO Ray Bayley, the range is based on the willingness of law firms to work collaboratively with Novus. Firms that take a passive-aggressive approach ("We still need to double-check your work") reduce the savings compared with firms that fully embrace Novus's expertise in the review process.

While document review is a huge part of the process expense in litigation, it is not the only process expense. If Novus's same process expertise and skill were brought to other aspects of the case (preparing discovery responses, for example), further savings would be available.

In addition to dealing with successful firms not wanting to change their approach, clients and third-party service providers like Novus must confront the "lawyers are special" mentality so prevalent in our profession. The argument is that only lawyers can review documents or can do the first draft of a document storyboard or discovery responses. This is rubbish, of course. Think about it in this light—if the document review involved a complex financial fraud, would you rather have it done by any person with a law degree from top law school or a trained forensic accountant? When you acknowledge that the accountant is the better choice, you've just acknowledged that a law degree is not essential to a variety of process-focused tasks.

---

48. Rachel M. Zahorsky and William D. Henderson, "Who's Eating Law Firms' Lunch?," *ABA Journal*, October 2013, 33.

The years since the Great Reset have demonstrated that lawyers are not "special" and that law firms are not immune from the principles that apply to every business. This period also has demonstrated what has always been true: that law is a buyers' market, save for very narrow projects or matters. Clients have a huge amount of power in pricing that they routinely fail to use. The tide seems to be turning on this point as well.

What does all of this mean? It means that change is happening— faster for some, slower for others. The first challenge is the "what if they're right?" challenge. How would a firm respond if its most significant client wanted it to price all matters on a fixed fee and begin driving the price down, year over year? The steps needed to do this might seem obvious, but behaviors are so ingrained that change cannot occur rapidly. Will clients wait while the firm figures that out?

For clients, the issues are even starker. Facing the "more with less" challenge without making significant changes is not going to happen. Achieving more with less requires a new mindset, a willingness to insist that your outside partners make material changes in the way they handle your work. Even if they are committed to changing to help you, it will not come easily, and the likelihood of falling back into bad habits is high. You will need to be diligent in ensuring that lawyers handling your matters stay committed to the new approach.

Your challenge is even greater though, because as noted earlier, lawyers cannot represent clients in ways that are at odds with their firm's values. Thus, you need to know the firm's values—for example, is it still compensating associates based in some part on hours and partners based on revenue? Those problems and others mean that you will not achieve the benefits you could with a fully committed partner.

For both law departments and firms, the change needed to thrive in the new normal will be significant. It will be a great distance from historic comfort zones. For that reason, it is important to take a look at change.

One way to look at it is to examine existing trends and simply "draw the line forward." The assumption is that change will occur at the same pace and in the same direction as it has been. Another way is to look for "weak signals"—what some are doing today that seems like it might catch on—and extrapolate them into the future. A third way is the reverse engineering scenario—envision the future and work backward to determine what must be done now to get to that point. The last way is the one where you can control the future.

The 50 percent (or 40 percent or 30 percent) challenge is real. It means the size of the pie available to lawyers is shrinking. Any shrinkage is bad news; significant shrinkage is a real problem and poses a real challenge. Some might choose to wait, hoping that Susskind's prediction is wrong and that legal spending once again starts increasing more than the rate of inflation. But if they are wrong, they will find themselves too far behind in the race to the future to survive intact. Those who choose to prepare for the future, who want to prevail in the combat for the hearts, minds, and wallets of clients, need to change significantly. Change is never easy, and in the context of law firms it presents a challenge unlike anything they have confronted before.

# Chapter 20
## MAKING CHANGE HAPPEN[49]

Usually change happens in one of four ways:

- It is announced.

- It is voted on and prevails.

- It happens spontaneously because something so dramatically frightens the incumbents that change becomes a necessity.

- It is distributed; that is, someone starts a change, and others adopt it until it develops enough momentum to sweep aside the past.

Which approach to change is likely to work in your business? They all have drawbacks.

- **No matter what they say, some people will simply oppose change.**

- **Others will simply oppose it by their indifference.**

- **Change that is voted in does not fare better.** While a majority voted for change, there are some who voted against it. Can you assume they will just give up and give in?

---

49. While this chapter focuses on changes from the position of inside counsel, those interested in changing their firms or practices should find plenty of grist for the mill.

- **Change that occurs because of a traumatic event may or may not work.** This approach is a poor one, and nobody should trigger the kind of cataclysmic event needed to motivate this kind of change. While some firms faced with imminent failure may change as a result of their near-death experience, hopefully most will approach the issue without the sense that a gun is pointed at their heads.

Finally, there is the distributed change—one at a time at first, and then more and more until, voila, the change has happened.

The best example of a distributed change is adopting e-mail. At first no lawyer was inclined to use such newfangled technology, and privilege issues were raised and threats made. Same with the use of cell phones. Now only the profession's dinosaurs do most of their work without e-mail or a smartphone. How did that change happen? Some lawyers bucked the status quo and found out how much better life was, and they acted as apostles and spread the word.

While firms and businesses are free to develop their own approach to change, it is important to keep in mind the human spirit. According to Wikipedia, inertia is "the resistance of any physical object to any change in its state of motion. . . ." Inertia is one of the most powerful forces influencing human behavior, and it is the primary demon you will have to overcome to achieve a better state. So if you agree that the status quo has room to improve, put yourself in this frame of mind: It's you versus inertia. If you don't do something, inertia wins. That is contrary to your best interests. Therefore, you are going to do some things differently to get the ball moving in the direction you want it to go. You will impose your will and overcome inertia.

Trying to develop the perfect approach to change is a waste of time and effort. Trying to make the new thing, whatever it might be, perfect is also a waste of time, particularly with lawyers, because nothing is ever perfect. Perfect is the enemy of better, so simply doing something better is a more enlightened approach.

With that mindset, here are some ideas to get you moving. You need not embrace all of these ideas. You need not embrace any of them. But you do need to embrace *an* idea so you *do something.* Doing nothing is a losing strategy for both clients and law firms.

**Figure 20.1**   Tips to Begin Change

| A. Get Your Mind Right | |
|---|---|
| **Clients** | **Law Firms/Lawyers** |
| 1. Don't wait. Embrace the ancient wisdom of Lao-tzu ("A journey of a thousand miles begins with a single step") and Einstein ("Insanity is doing the same thing over and over and expecting a different result"). | Same. |
| 2. Identify a change coach. Change is hard. It is harder when you do it alone. Think about working out on your own or working out with a trainer—which is more effective? You will do better when you are accountable to someone. Identify that person. Call her or him *today.* | Same. |
| 3. Talk to your colleagues about what you learned in this book. In your company, the CFO counts. | Use lunches to find colleagues who share your thinking. |
| 4. Look over your portfolio of law firms and identify one that appears to be a change leader. Call and schedule a meeting. | Think about each of your clients, and identify one who appears interested in trying to do things differently. Call and schedule a meeting. |
| **B. Create Your Vision** | |
| 1. Identify your biggest pain points with outside counsel. | Identify things you could do better and things your client could do better that would enhance the value of your services. |

**Figure 20.1** (continued)

| | |
|---|---|
| 2. Rank on a scale of 1 to 10 the importance of (a) reducing your legal spend, (b) increasing predictability of your legal spend, and (c) gaining better results faster. | Ask your client to do the ranking in the Client column at left (if it hasn't already been done), and make sure you know how the client ranked the priorities. |
| 3. Communicate the results of number 2 to your outside lawyers so they can help you achieve these results. | Make sure you always ask about the client's issues in number 2 so that your client knows you are thinking about them. |
| 4. Identify five changes needed to develop a better-performing law department, and assess how you accomplish each of them. | Identify five changes needed to develop a better-performing law firm/practice group, and assess how you accomplish each of them. |
| 5. Make a timetable for each of the five changes identified in number 4. Develop a system to track your progress. | Same. |
| **C. The Power of Two** | |
| 1. Identify two new (or newish) cases. Define success. Tell your outside counsel. | Identify two new (or newish) cases. Define success. Call your client and find out if your definitions match. |
| 2. Identify two different cases. Create project charters for both. | Identify two different cases. Create project charters for both. Ask for your client's opinion. |
| 3. Pick two new cases and do early case assessments for both. | Pick two new cases and do early case assessments for both. Share with your client. |
| 4. Identify two ordinary cases. Ask your outside lawyer to propose a value-based fee. | Identify two ordinary cases. Propose a value-based fee to your client. |
| 5. Use value fees on two cases within sixty days. | Same. |
| 6. Use value fees on two more cases within 120 days. | Same. |

**Figure 20.1**   (continued)

| D. Learn More | |
|---|---|
| 1. Find a blog or column that regularly contains information on value fees. Subscribe. | Find a blog or column that regularly contains information on value fees. Subscribe. Send key posts to your client. |
| 2. Read *The Checklist Manifesto* by Atul Gawande and determine where checklists will work for you. | Same. |
| 3. Prepare a checklist. | Same. |
| 4. Investigate how high-functioning groups like the Navy SEALs end their missions and why they end them that way. | Same. |
| 5. Attend ACC's Legal Services Management program or ask ACC to provide training for your department and key outside counsel. | Attend ACC's Legal Services Management program or ask ACC to provide training for your colleagues. Share what you learned with your client. |
| **E. Make Your Firms (Clients) Your Partners** | |
| 1. Have three of your firms prepare project charters. Work with them on improving the charters. | Prepare project charters on cases for three clients. Work with clients on improving the charters. |
| 2. Demand alternative budgets on a case—a task-based budget and an experience-driven budget. | Prepare alternative budgets on a case—a task-based budget and an experience-driven budget. Measure how you perform to budget even if your client doesn't. |
| 3. Ask your firm's lawyers to identify five things in the budget they could live without. Then ask for five more. | Identify five things in the budget you think you and your client could live without. Then identify five more. Ask for your client's opinion about not having these tasks within the scope of work. |
| 4. Tell all of your firms handling repeat work that you want to discuss value fees for your next budget year. | When you are handling repeat work, tell your client that you want to discuss value fees for your next budget year. |

**Figure 20.1**   (continued)

| F. Become a Pied Piper | |
|---|---|
| 1. Ask your outside counsel to send you every example of businesses having success with value-based fees. | Send your client every example of businesses having success with value-based fees. |
| 2. Share these stories with your colleagues and your other outside firms. | Share these stories with your colleagues. |
| 3. Celebrate your company's "wins" in this area, both internally and by sharing the win with your outside lawyers. | Celebrate your firm's "wins" in this area, both internally and by sharing the win with your firm's clients. |
| 4. Schedule regular department meetings to discuss progress in adopting value-based fees. | Same. |
| 5. Require after-action assessments on all matters. | Conduct after-action assessments on all matters. |
| **G. Don't Reinvent the Wheel** | |
| 1. "Borrow" a form for after-action assessments. Tailor it to suit your needs. | Same. |
| 2. Peruse the ACC Value Challenge website and borrow any useful material. | Same. |
| 3. Invite knowledgeable people to a lunch with you and your colleagues to learn from them. | Same. |
| 4. Ask your firms to share their checklists with you and your other firms. | Share your checklists with your clients. Be a team player—invite them to share these checklists with their other firms. |
| 5. Commit to reporting your progress publicly. Doing so will help you stay on track. | Same. |

Einstein famously said, "We cannot solve our problems with the same thinking we used when we created them." Steve Jobs told Apple employees to "Think Different." It's now up to you—think BIG. When you create a big target, make it BIGGER. If you think you can reduce your legal spend by 20 percent, why not imagine doing so by 40 percent? Or more? The limits on success are only those you choose to accept.

Now get to work.

*"There are three rules for writing a [book].*
*Unfortunately, nobody knows what they are."*

—W. Somerset Maugham

In case there is a second edition of this book, feel free to send questions or suggestions for improvement to patrick.lamb@valoremlaw.com.

# Appendix

"Here's to the crazy ones—the misfits, the rebels, the trouble-makers, the round pegs in the square holes. The ones who see things differently—they're not fond of rules and they have no respect for the status quo. You can quote them, disagree with them, glorify or vilify them, but the only thing you can't do is ignore them, because they change things. They push the human race forward, and while some may see them as the crazy ones, we see genius, because the people who are crazy enough to think they can change the world are the ones who do."

——Steve Jobs

The Appendix contains the following samples:
- After-Action Assessment Sample
- Checklist Sample
- Early Case Assessment
- Engagement Letter Sample
- Pricing Checklist

# AFTER-ACTION ASSESSMENT SAMPLE

## AFTER-ACTION ASSESSMENT

Matter: _____           Date: _____

| Topic | What Went Well | Take a Look At |
|---|---|---|
| People/Staffing | | |
| Technology | | |
| Strategy | | |
| Communication | | |
| Outcome | | |
| Reserve setting | | |
| Other | | |

| | | |
|---|---|---|
| Top takeaways: Valorem | 1. | 2. |
| Top takeaways: [Name of Client] | 1. | 2. |

| | |
|---|---|
| [Client] happiness score/comment | |
| Did [client] personnel reflect [client] values? | |
| Did Valorem personnel reflect [client] values? | |

| | |
|---|---|
| Greatest opportunity for improvement: Client | |
| Greatest opportunity for improvement: Valorem | |

# CHECKLIST SAMPLE

## JURY TRIAL CHECKLIST (Last Revised 3-2013)

| Issue: Jury Selection | Explanation |
|---|---|
| Determine number of jurors to be seated for trial | |
| Determine number of alternates to be seated | |
| Determine if verdict must be unanimous | |
| Trial time estimate—push low | This relates to the number of days the jury venire will be told to expect the trial to last. Most trials are shorter than expected, but critically most employers will pay for no more than 10 days of jury service. If trial estimate is longer, many employed potential jurors will we excused. |
| Number of prospective jurors on the venire brought into court | |
| Determine if court uses juror form. If yes, determine availability of completed forms | Some courts allow lawyers to obtain copies, sometimes for a fee. *Have check available.* |
| Determine how court selects prospective jurors from the venire panel to populate the jury box for questioning. Random or sequential order. | Critical to determine if you can tell "who's next" from jurors not sitting in jury box. |
| Number of prospective jurors to be seated in the box at one time | |
| Number of prospective jurors to be questioned at one time | |
| Obtain number system for jurors seated in jury box | |

| | |
|---|---|
| Confirm whether voir dire by lawyers allowed? | |
| Rules on using juror names? | |
| Confirm no exhibits shown during voir dire | |
| Confirm no discussion of case specific facts | |
| Any rules on scope of questions allowed | |
| "Good for goose/gander" rule? | If one side starts asking questions of a certain type without objection, does that mean that the other side can ask same types of questions without objections being sustained? |
| Number of preemptory challenges per side | |
| When and how will for cause challenges be considered? | What order? Outside the presence of the venire? Before peremptory challenges? |
| Are preemptories announced to the jury or to the court? | Do you have to stand up and say "We would like to thank and excuse Juror Number _____"? |
| Does the court permit strike backs? | For a detailed discussion of this issue, see http://www.juryblog.com/the-trial-lawyers-rights/right-to-back-strike/ |
| Are alternates selected separately? | Do they know they are alternates during trial? |
| Additional preemptories for alternates? | |

| | |
|---|---|
| Request pre-instruction to entire venire that:<br><br>• Do no speak to parties or lawyers until case is over<br><br>• Do not perform any research on the internet, or elsewhere about the issues, the parties or the lawyers<br><br>• Not permitted to speak to lawyers<br><br>• Not permitted to speak to each other or others about the case | |
| Rules for voir dire? | Speak from seat or stand? Movement allowed? |
| **Issue: Rules for Opening** | **Explanation** |
| Can exhibits be used? | |
| Can PowerPoint or Elmo be used? | Approval of other side required?<br><br>If objection, does court rule or simply no use? |
| Who provides AV equipment? | Shared use? |
| Demonstratives OK? | Procedures for preapproval? |
| Time limits? | |
| Where to stand? Movement allowed? Is podium available? Is its use required? | |
| Allowed to refer to matters that are the subject of MIL or objection? | |
| **Issue: Rules for Exhibits** | **Explanation** |
| Pare down lists even if no prejudice is engendered? | Parties should know what is likely to be used. |

| | |
|---|---|
| Move exhibits into evidence individually or at end of witness testimony but before witness is excused? | Does latter affect ability to publish to the jury? (Do not suggest or agree to en masse motion to admit because reduces chance of objections being granted and eliminates ability to use witness to correct foundation deficiencies.) |
| Is permission required to publish any admitted exhibit? | |
| Premark exhibits? Any preferences on numbering? | |
| Court permission required to approach witness to show exhibit? | |
| Permissible for lawyers to highlight documents, call out paragraphs, or otherwise mark documents on screen? | |
| **Issue: Objections** | **Explanation** |
| Should counsel stand to make objections? | |
| Ask court to commit to how much (little) in terms of speaking objections the court will permit in presence of the jury. | |
| Does court use sidebars? If not, how/ when are you permitted to make record on objections and rulings? | |
| Can counsel raise with the court outside the presence of the jury before the morning session begins (or other defined time) any issues that have arisen? If so, what is the proper procedure to alert the court of an issue that requires an "outside the presence" conference? | |

| Issue: Miscellaneous | Explanation |
|---|---|
| Are jurors allowed to take notes? | |
| Are jurors allowed to ask questions? If yes, how does this process work? | |
| Does the court ask questions of the witnesses? | |
| Any pet peeves the court has about trial lawyer behavior or practices? | |
| Is there a standard order barring witnesses from the courtroom before their testimony? | |
| Is there a 24-hour rule or some other standard practice for identifying upcoming witness order? | |
| Does the court allow witnesses to be called out of order if scheduling problems arise? | |
| Does the court reporter provide real-time transcripts? Are dirty dailies available? Typically by what time? | |
| Alert court to issues expected to come up during trial | Don't argue unless invited. Just flag the issue. |

# EARLY CASE ASSESSMENT

## Litigation Assessment

Date First Prepared: _____

Last Updated: _____

## Summary:

| | |
|---|---|
| Claimant Name: | Venue: |
| In-House Lawyer: | Docket No.: |
| Outside Lawyers Assigned: *[Firm, Lead Counsel]* | Date Filed: *[Including Amendment Dates]* |
| Decision Tree Attached? | |
| Mediation Candidate? | Judge *[Arbitration panel in the case of arbitration]*: |
| Budget Amount: | Opposing Counsel: |
| Budget Attached? | Settlement Value: |

**Is there anything that makes this case special or unusual?**

From management's perspective? _____

From the law department's perspective? _____

From the business unit's perspective? _____

From a public relations perspective? _____

## The Team:

Inside Counsel: _____

Outside Counsel: _____

Business Unit Responsible: _____

Business Unit Contact: _____

## The Claim:

**A.** Description of Matter:

**B.** Type of Case:

☐ Antitrust ☐ Securities ☐ Environmental

☐ Contract ☐ Product Liability

☐ Employment ☐ General Tort

**C.** Named Defendants:

☐ Parent ☐ Officers ☐ Vendors

☐ Subsidiary ☐ Directors

Which one? ☐ Customers

**D.** Key Issues:

[*Identify, with specificity, the critical (outcome determinative) issues in the case.*]

## Risk Management:

**A.** All or any parties of claim insured?

_____ Yes _____ No

• Who made the decision?

**B.** If yes, have all potentially applicable policies been located?

_____ Yes _____ No

**C.** If no, who is responsible for locating all potentially applicable policies? _____

**D.** Has notice been sent to all carriers potentially on the risk?

_____ Yes _____ No

• Who sent notice?

• On what date?

**E.** Carrier response to notice: _____

**F.** Reporting requirement: _____

## Our Adversary:

**A.** Do we have an ongoing business relationship with our adversary?

_____ Yes   _____ No

If yes, what is the annual amount?

(Anything over $_____ requires business approval of case strategy.)

**B.** Is our adversary a person _____ or corporation _____?

If a corporation, what is its annual revenue? _____

**C.** Opposing counsel: _____

Reputation? _____

**D.** Inside contact identified: _____

**E.** Key Issues: _____

[*Identify, with specificity, the key (outcome determination) issues in the case.*]

## Case Evaluation:

**1.** Provide an assessment of each of the allegations and alleged damages. Assessment should address, for example, likelihood of success, including percentages. Any decision tree or similar analysis should be incorporated into the plan.

**2.** Assess opposing counsel.

**3.** Assess venue.

**4.** What is the settlement value of the case?

**5.** What is the worst possible risk to the company (90 percent certainty)?

## Overall Disposition Strategy:

[*Provide a brief statement of the overall disposition strategy for the matter. This should include a brief statement of what the primary*] *objective is; i.e., trying, settling, or dismissing the case, and the timetable to reach the primary objective.*]

Mediation required by contract? _____

Arbitration clause? _____

## Detail Strategy:

1. **Discovery Objectives:** [*Describe the objective of each phase during discovery and within each phase where appropriate (e.g., individual to be deposed).*]

2. **Anticipated Discovery Problems:**

3. **Electronic Discovery Issues:**

4. **Motions:**

   [*a. Explain, for each motion anticipated, the objective, the discovery necessary, the schedule, and the effect of the motion on the overall strategy.*

   *b. Explain anticipated motions by opposition and strategy for responding.*]

5. **Experts:**

   [*a. Describe each expert needed in the litigation for which issues, and, if possible, recommend specific individuals.*

   *b. Describe types of anticipated experts for opposition.*]

6. **Trial:**

   [*a. Describe the strategy for proceeding to trial, the likely phases of the trial, and the schedule.*

   *b. Assess the likelihood of trial.*]

7. **Settlement, Mediation, or Other ADR:** [*Virtually all cases resolve. Explain settlement strategy, including assessment of likelihood of settlement, and the strategy for positioning case for settlement.*]

   • Does contract at issue require mediation?

   _____ Yes        _____ No

If yes, attach relevant provision.

## Lawyers On The Case:

*[For each lawyer on the case, attach the lawyer's bio and indicate here each lawyer's role in the case. Lawyers who are not listed here are not permitted to bill time to this matter without [CLIENT'S] consent.]*

APPROVED:                                    SUBMITTED BY:

[CLIENT]

_____          _____

**Name**                                            Lead Outside Lawyer:

**Date:** _____

**Modifications** noted:

**Date:** _____    _____          _____

          [CLIENT]                          Lead Outside Lawyer

## Litigation Assessment

(Repetitive Litigation Addendum)

How many similar cases have been filed against [CLIENT]? _____

What is the company's settlement history with this
type of case? _____

      Average settlement _____

      High settlement _____

      Low settlement _____

What is the average number of days from filing to resolution? _____

Has [CLIENT] litigated claims against the plaintiff's lawyer before?

_____

If yes, provide information regarding the nature of claims litigated
and settlement history:

Are there any special facts that make this case unusual?

# ENGAGEMENT LETTER SAMPLE

*Direct Dial: 312-676-5462*

*patrick.lamb@valoremlaw.com*

[Date]

Via e-mail/U.S. mail

Jane Smith, Esq.
Executive Vice President and General Counsel
ABC Corporation
123 Main Street
Everywhere, IL 60400

Re:  *Evil Empire Inc. v. ABC Corporation*
    Valorem Law Group Engagement Letter

Dear Jane:

Thank you for engaging Valorem to represent ABC in the Evil Empire matter currently pending before the United States District Court for the Northern District of Illinois. We greatly appreciate the opportunity to work with you and your team. This letter confirms the terms of our engagement based on our telephone conversations.

**Our Fee:** We have agreed to a fixed fee of $xxx,xxx.00, to be paid in two installments. The first installment, $yy,yyy.00, is due within ten days of your execution of this letter. This installment covers all work, scoped and described in Exhibit A, through the end of written discovery. The second installment for the balance will be due when depositions commence or 120 days from now, whichever is later. The second installment covers the work that is scoped and described in Exhibit A and concludes with the filing of the summary judgment response or reply briefs, or ninety days before trial, whichever is later. If needed, ABC and Valorem will agree on a fee for trial preparation and trial in advance of the time that work will be required.

The first payment is nonrefundable. If the matter settles or is otherwise resolved before the second payment is due, it will not be due or owed. Once the second payment is made, it is nonrefundable. Upon receipt of each payment, Valorem shall account for the payment as firm revenue. To the extent that work becomes required or merits consideration that is not set forth in Exhibit A, we will work with you to determine whether the fee should be adjusted or whether you wish to bear the risk of forgoing the additional work.

In addition to the fixed fee, ABC will be responsible for out-of-pocket costs incurred during the litigation, such as travel, couriers, experts (if necessary), court reporter fees, and so forth. We do not mark up our out-of-pocket costs. These costs will be billed to you monthly, and payment should be made within thirty days of your receipt of the invoice.

We have agreed to a holdback of 20 percent of our fee. This amount will be placed in a client fund account. At the conclusion of the matter, when the outcome and value of our work is known, you will decide whether we are entitled to some, all, none, or a multiple of the total in the holdback account. The award of the holdback will be entirely within your discretion.

**Staffing:** This matter will be staffed by Nicole Auerbach, Margot Klein, and me, as well as one of our paralegals, Sarah Houdek. Biographies of our team members are attached as Exhibit B.

**Termination:** We are hopeful of a long relationship with ABC and will strive to become your litigators of choice. We wish to advise you, however, that you are entitled to terminate our engagement at any time, for any reason. If you do, per the agreement on fees, no fees will be refunded or due to ABC. We have the right to withdraw from representing ABC. If we withdraw, we will refund to ABC an amount of fees paid that we believe is fairly allocable to any work not performed under the applicable section of Exhibit A. If we withdraw or you terminate our engagement, ABC will remain obligated to pay for all costs incurred on behalf of ABC.

Please note your acceptance of this engagement by signing below and returning a signed copy to my attention. As always, if you have questions about any of these matters or any other aspect of our relationship, please let me know.

Jane, we are so excited to have the chance to provide services to ABC, and we will endeavor to provide you a basis for believing our engagement was one of your best decisions.

Sincerely,

VALOREM LAW GROUP, LLP

Patrick J. Lamb

AGREED & ACCEPTED:

**ABC Corporation**

**By:** _____

**Date:** _____

# PRICING CHECKLIST

| | Pricing | Impact in this matter | Variability | Up/down/- |
|---|---|---|---|---|
| **Case issues** | | | | |
| 1 | Number of parties | | | |
| 2 | Expected time to trial | | | |
| 3 | Expected stops and starts | | | |
| 4 | Forum | | | |
| 5 | Knowledge of opposing counsel | | | |
| 6 | Significant legal issues | | | |
| 7 | Span of time at issue | | | |
| 8 | Number of depositions | | | |
| 9 | Document volume (all parties) | | | |
| 10 | Factual complexity | | | |
| 11 | E-discovery issues | | | |
| 12 | Likelihood of success on merits | | | |
| **Firm issues** | | | | |
| 13 | Case staffing required | | | |
| 14 | What % each person's capacity? | | | |
| 15 | Firm capacity | | | |
| 16 | Opportunities lost? | | | |
| 17 | Cash flow certainty | | | |

| Client Issues | | | | |
|---|---|---|---|---|
| 18 | Existing client | | | |
| 19 | Potential for repeat work? | | | |
| 20 | Happiness factor | | | |
| 21 | Clarity of objectives | | | |
| 22 | Reasonable re settlement? | | | |
| 23 | Attitudes re disaggregation | | | |
| 24 | Business dynamics—other party | | | |
| 25 | Risk tolerance | | | |
| 26 | Importance of case to client | | | |
| 27 | High maintenance? | | | |
| **Miscellaneous** | | | | |
| 28 | Identity of competitors | | | |
| 29 | Competitor pricing | | | |
| 30 | Create conflicts of concern? | | | |
| **Variation** | | | | |
| 31 | Top 3 factors increasing cost | | | |
| 32 | Likelihood of 31 | | | |
| 33 | Top 3 factors lowering cost | | | |
| 34 | Likelihood of 33 | | | |
| **Most important factors in this matter** | | | | |

# Index

## A

ABA Model Rules of Professional
Conduct, 127–133, 138–139
accounting issues. *See also* client trust
accounts
client trust accounts, 123–124,
138–139
with holdbacks, 124–125
with retainer agreements, 123–124
ACC's Legal Services Management
program, 159
ACC Value Challenge, 2, 160
ACES system, 23, 29
advance payment retainer agreements,
124
after-action assessments, 93–98
opportunities for improvement,
identifying, 95
sample form, 164
shared experiences, learning from, 95
STEALTH debriefs, 96–97
virtuous circle, 96
allocation of resources, 57, 75–76, 114
early decisions and, 61
alternative budgets, 159
alternative fee arrangements (AFAs)
as alternative to hourly billing, 17
calculation of, firm-focused, 141–142

case-handling methods, 143–144
client dissatisfaction with, 14
client focus, questioning, 142–146
comparing with hours-based billing,
39–40
contingency fees, 22–23. *See also*
contingency fees
engagement letters, 47–51
expectations of, 12
fixed fees, 21–22. *See also* fixed fees
hybrid fee agreements, 23–24
issues of, 39–51
perceived effectiveness at cost
reduction, 6
perceived effectiveness vs. actual
impact, 5
pricing, 107–122
results achieved focus, 46
retainer agreements, 20–21. *See also*
retainer agreements
reverse contingency fees, 23
as surrogate for hourly billing, 13–14
unrealized potential of, xi–xii, 11
value provision, 16. *See also* value
alternative legal service providers, 91
Novus Law, 87–91
*American Lawyer*, 8

assessments after the action, 93–98
associates
    compensation and advancement, 43
    costs in blended rates, 19
    costs of, 42, 143
    hours vs. efficiency of, 145
    pressures on, 24–25
    training and turnover costs, 7
assumptions
    about firms as rational economic
        actors, 20
    about pace of change, 154
    about time as measure of value, 120
    basing pricing on, 120
    of fee agreements, 48, 120
    of hourly billing model, 39–40
*At the Intersection* (Woldow), 64n
automatic tasks, 69–70

# B

Baker, Ronald J., 149–150
Bartlit, Fred, 57, 68, 108–109, 111
Bartlit Beck, 57, 68, 108–109
Bayley, Ray, 68–69, 152
behavior
    client influence on, xv, 23
    incentives driving, 24–25
    as incentivized by fee structures, 17,
        22, 24, 26, 32
    as incentivized by profitability, 45–46
    as incentivized by time-based billing,
        20
    ingrained behavior and change, 153,
        156
BHAG (Big Hairy Audacious Goal),
    104n
billable hours. *See also* hourly rates
    alternatives to, 17. *See also* alternative
        fee arrangements (AFAs)
    charading as alternative fees, 13
    ethical considerations, 131
    ingrained in law firm DNA, 14
    as measure of performance, 43
    overreliance on, 7
    problems with, 6–7
billing
    vs. collection, 3–4

cost-plus billing, 17
    price-led costing, 149–152
billing structures
    AFAs, 20–24
    not AFAs, 18–20
blended rates, 5–6, 18–19
bonuses, 26, 30
    criteria defining, 47
    on fixed fee cases, 22
    for number of hours worked, 42
Bryant, Bear, 63
budgeting engagements, 23
budgets
    alternative budgets, 159
    deferred payments and, 102
    fiscal or calendar, 102
    planning and managing, 71
    risks, assessing, 71
business dynamics
    assessing, 59
    influence on pricing, 116
business knowledge, 16
business planning with fixed fees, 15
business units
    fee charged to, 102
    interviewing, 59
    perspective on case, 170
    value of certainty to, 102

# C

capacity for work, influence on pricing,
    116
capped fees, 5, 19–20
    defined, 18–20
    with shared savings, 23–24
Carr, Jeffrey, xiii–xiv, 23, 110
Carville, James, 99
case cycle time, 15–16
    reductions in, 114
case dimensions, influence on pricing, 115
case locale, influence on pricing, 115
cases
    alternative budgets for, 159
    corpus of facts, 59–60
    critical thinking during, 58–59
    odds of winning, 77
    project management, applicability

of, 71
risk and spend, understanding,
    83–84
risks of, 57
settlement worth, 77
value of, 77
cash flow analysis, influence on pricing,
    117
certainty
    about revenue, 107–108
    with ACES system, 23
    of fees and value, 31
    with fixed fees, 22, 132
    lawyer fear of fixed fees and, 109–110
    leveling, 21
    premium paid for, 84
    as valued by business units, 102
    as valued by clients, 122, 133, 142
chance of winning case analysis, 78
change
    approaches to, 155, 157–161
    championing, 160
    distributed change, 155–156
    drawbacks to, 155–156
    vs. inertia, 156–157
    learning how, 159
    mindset for, 157
    partnering with clients or firms for,
        159
    power of two, 158
    in preparation for future, 147–154
    rate of, 33–35
    reusing and sharing knowledge, 160
    vision of, 157–158
change coaches, 157
change curve, 34–35
change order approval, 49
*Checklist Manifesto: How to Get Things
    Right, The* (Gawande), 72, 159
checklists, 73–76, 159
    client taste for, 103
    for pricing, 179–180
    sample checklist, 73–75, 165–169
    sharing, 160
    topics for, 75
churn, 5, 8, 148
civil cases, ethics of value-based fees,
    136–137

classic retainer agreements, 123
client attention, influence on pricing, 115
client attitude, influence on pricing, 116
client communication. *See* lawyer-client
    communication
client expectations, managing, 71
client experience, 99–105
    client service, 100–101
    headaches, identifying, 102
    Lean or Six Sigma, incorporating,
        102
    tailoring to client needs, 102–104
client goals and objectives, 27
    influence on pricing, 116
client personality, influence on pricing,
    116
client position, critical thinking about,
    57–59
client relationships, 99–100
    influence on pricing, 115–116
client risk tolerance, influence on pricing,
    116
clients
    ability to pay, 133
    accounting issues, 124–125
    billable hours, view of, 15–16
    checklists, taste for, 103
    commitment to early knowledge, 112
    cost of production, reducing for,
        53–54
    disaggregation, taste for, 103
    diversity, commitment to, 102
    face-to-face meetings with, 104
    financial relationship with law firms,
        4
    new vs. repeat, 108
    power in pricing, 152–153
    predictability needs, 41
    questions to ask about AFA
        proposals, 142–146
    risk assessments, 83–84
    satisfaction of, 4
    trust in lawyers, 46, 122
    work value to, 104–105
client trust accounts
    for client protection, 139
    depositing funds in and withdrawing
        from, 123–124, 139

flat and fixed fees, depositing in, 138
Clifford, Clark, 120–121
Clinton, Bill, 99
collection vs. billing, 3–4
combined claim value analysis, 79–80
commercial expectations, influence on
    pricing, 118
competent representation, 130
competitor pricing, influence on pricing,
    116
complexification, xiii–xiv
contingency fees, 22–23, 111
    advantages and drawbacks, 29
    in civil cases, 136–137
    functions of, 131
    lawyer risk in, 137
    reasonableness of, 137–138
    reasonable use of, 137
continuous learning, 96
contracts, evaluation criteria, 102
convergence programs, 1
Corcoran, Tim, 100
corporate counsel. See also in-house
    counsel; law departments
    in-house work, 4
corpus of facts, 59–60
costing, price-led, 149–152
cost-plus pricing, 17, 150–151
    cost reduction and, 71
cost reductions, 114
    perceived effectiveness of AFAs, 6
    tools for. See tools for lowering
        production costs
costs of service/production, xii–xiii
    after-action assessments, lowering
        with, 96
    cost savings with outsourcing, 152
    doing less and, 84
    profitability and, 42
    reducing, 12–13, 53–54. See also
        tools for lowering production
        costs
    time influences on, 118
    time to knowledge, accelerating, 111
CounselLink report, 2
Court of Appeals for the District of
    Columbia on flat fees, 131–132, 140
Covey, Stephen, 149

Craxton, Harold, 63
critical thinking curves, 58–59
customer service. See also client experience
    commitment to, 30
    evolution of, 100
    value fees and, 105
cycle time, 15–16
    influence on pricing, 115
    reductions in, 114

**D**

Damon, Lisa, 6
D.C. Circuit Court of Appeals on flat fees,
    131–132, 140
Debrief Imperative, The (Duke and
    Murphy), 94, 96
debriefs, 93–98
decision making
    allocation of resources and, 61
    with less information, 84
    time to knowledge and, 111–112
DecisionPro software, 80n
decision trees, 77–81
    analysis of personal injury case,
        78–79
    50 percent chance of winning, 78
    software for, 80
    value of combined claim, 79–80
deliverables, 70
    costs of, 71. See also costs of service/
        production
depositions
    after disaggregated document review,
        91
    preparing for, task sequencing, 68, 70
    pricing as phase of case, 22
diligence, structure of fees and, 130
disaggregation, 85–91
    client taste for, 103
    for document review process, 87–91
    strategy for, 144–145
discounted hourly rates, 18
discounts, 1
discovery disputes, 48
distributed change, 155–156
District of Columbia Bar Legal Ethics
    Comm., Op. 355, on earned fees,

138–139
diversity, demonstrating, 102
DLA Piper, 8–9
document review
    accuracy, delivery, and cost in, 88
    disaggregation of, 87–91
    expense of, 85–86
    importance of, 86
    one-touch system for, 90
    outsourcing, 144–145
    process of, 70
    process of, engineering, 86–87
    third-party vendors for, 87
documents of essential case issues,
    analyzing, 59–60
*Dowling v. Chicago Options Associate, Inc.*,
    124
Drucker, Peter, 150–151
Duke, William, 94, 96

# E

early case assessment (ECA), 57–62
    addressing in engagement letters, 49
    allocation of resources and, 61
    costs of, 60
    critical thinking curves, 58–59
    direct information process, 60–61
    features of, 59
    importance of, 61
    opportunities for errors, 60–61
    sample form, 170–175
early decisions, allocation of resources
    and, 61
e-discovery
    influence on pricing, 117
    tools for, 86
efficiency
    billable hours and, 7
    checklists for, 72–76
    of knowledge gains, 112
    project management for, 63–72
    with value-based fees, 15, 132
    value of, 42, 145
Eighth Circuit Court of Appeals, *Little
    Rock School Dist. v. Arkansas*,
    134–135
Einstein, Albert, 7, 51, 157, 161

e-mails, as essential documents in cases,
    59–60
*End of Lawyers?: Rethinking the Nature
    of Legal Services, The* (Susskind), 35,
    147n
engagement letters
    assumptions of fee arrangement,
        specifying, 48
    change order approval criteria, 49
    early case assessment requirements,
        49
    expert fees, addressing, 50
    fee structure, setting, 46
    full disclosure, 51
    local counsel fees, addressing, 50
    outside expenditures approval
        process, 49
    sample letter, 176–178
    staffing, defining, 47–48
    terms, specifying, 47–51
    timing of bills and payments,
        specifying, 48
    trial and trial preparation fees,
        addressing, 50
    volume discounts, addressing, 50–51
    what-ifs, addressing, 49–50
    work to be performed, specifying,
        48–49
engagements
    client expectations, 104
    profitability, determining, 42
    quality metrics, 42
    scope of, changing, 49
enhancements, value-based, 134–135
error reduction, 65, 97
escrow, 138
ethical considerations, 127–140
    in civil context, 136–137
    of flat fees, 138–140
    philosophy of ABA Model Rules,
        131–132
    reasonable fees, 133–135
    of structuring value-based fees,
        128–131
expert fees, including in fee arrangement,
    50

# F

face-to-face meetings, 104
fact accumulation
    streamlined process, 67
    traditional process, 66–67
failures, learning from, 93–95
fairness, 122
    concerns about, 29
    expectations of, 12
federal fee-shifting statutes, 134–135
Federal Rules of Civil Procedure
    on document review, 86
    Rule 33(d)(1), 91
fee calculation, xiv. *See also* pricing
fee collars, 24, 29
fees
    assumptions underlying, 48
    awarded by court, 134–135
    "earned," 138–139
    fixed fees. *See* fixed fees
    hourly fees. *See* hourly rates
    past pricing, 112–113
    reasonable fees, 128, 133–135
    setting, 46
    tied to outcomes, 45
fee-shifting statutes, 134–135
fee structures
    advantages and drawbacks of, 28–29
    aligning with objectives, 27, 32
    behavior incentivized by, 17, 24
    for competent representation, 130
    deferred payments, 102
    ethical considerations, 127–140
    modification of, 30
    overlays on, 25–26, 30
*Fifth Discipline, The* (Senge), 97
50 percent challenge, 147–154
filings, draft review, 103
Fireman's Fund Insurance, 90
fixed fees, 5, 14, 21–22, 53–54
    advantages and drawbacks, 28–29
    bonuses and holdbacks, 22, 30–31
    business planning with, 15
    hours-based, 40–41
    multiple cases by time, 22
    opinions about, 109
    phases of cases, 22
    portfolios of cases, 21
    pricing equation, 40
    recognizing as revenue, 124
    single cases, 21
    single cases by time, 22
    uncertainty and, 109–111
    value, certainty, and, 31
Flaherty, D. Casey, 37
flat fees, 5
    disbursal, 138–140
    ethical considerations, 138–140
    functions of, 131–132
    milestones for earning, 139
FMC Technologies, xiii–xiv, 23, 110
future, preparing for, 147–154

# G

Gawande, Atul, 72, 159
GDP, legal expenditures as percentage
    of, 2
Gleeson, Brent, 93–94
Grady, Ken, 147, 149
Great Reset, 11–12
    efficiency and predictability demands
    of, 33
Greenspan, Steven, 6
Grumbine, David, 15
guaranteed dollars vs. uncertain dollars,
    107–108

# H

Hassett, Jim, 64n, 70
historic costs, reducing, 143. *See also* cost
    reductions
historic data, mining for pricing
    information, 112–114
holdbacks, 22, 25–26
    accounting issues, 124–125
    client service commitment and, 30
    criteria for, 47
    effort expended and, 30
    influence on pricing, 117
    performance and, 32, 109
hourly rate mentality, 43, 51, 145–146
hourly rates, 53
    alternative fees as surrogate for,
    13–14

alternatives to, xiv. *See also* alternative
    fee arrangements (AFAs)
annual growth in, 2–3
client's view of, 15
cutting, 2
defined, 18
pricing equation, 40
problems with, 6–7, 11
profit margin, 39, 110
hours, as firm-facing metric, 108
Huron Consulting, 33
hybrid fee agreements, 23–24

**I**

Illinois Supreme Court on retainer
    agreements, 123
improvement opportunities, identifying,
    95
incremental costs, 108
inertia vs. change, 156–157
in-house counsel
    and outside lawyers, strain between,
        35
    value to teams, 105
*In re Mance*, 139–140
*In Search of Excellence* (Peters and
    Waterman), 100
invoices
    as lagging indicators of work, 46
    Value Adjustment Line, viii, 105, 121

**J**

Jessen, Nancy, 33
Jobs, Steve, 161
Johnston, Deanna, 90
jury selection checklist, 73–75, 165–169

**K**

Kaizen, 64
key innovations of legal profession, 36
Kia Motors, 37
Kirkland & Ellis, 68
knowledge, time to, 111–118
Kurzweil, Ray, 34

**L**

Lao-tzu, 157
law
    as business vs. profession, 37, 43
    as buyer's market, 153
    Lean Six Sigma activities, 65
law departments
    budget goals, 103
    case-handling processes, 103
    change needed for new normal,
        152–154
    fees charged to, 102
    growth in, 35
    legal spend reductions, 147–148
law department supervisors, 102
law firms
    aligning with clients, 42–43
    behavior or. *See* behavior
    as businesses, 43
    certainty vs. value, 31
    change needed in, 148–149, 152–154
    churn, 5, 8, 148
    economic upheaval in, 2
    expenses, primary, 13
    financial relationship with clients, 4
    history of case pricing, 112–113
    hourly model mentality, 43, 51,
        145–146
    incremental costs, 108
    and law departments, gap between,
        35
    partner mobility, 5, 8, 148
    personnel as cost item, 13, 115
    profitability, generation of, 12–13
    profitability vs. revenue, 9
    real estate as cost item, 13
    revenue, focus on, 25
    revenue rankings, 8
    rising costs, 2
    value provision, 14, 83. *See also* value
    values of, influence on client
        representation, 153
    windfalls, 44, 120–121
lawyer-client communication
    with decision trees, 80–81
    ethical issues, resolving through,
        130–131
    facilitating, 15–16

of foreseeable pitfalls and risks, 133
managing, 71
of structure of fee arrangement,
129–130
of triggers for earned fees, 140
lawyers
business judgment, 33
client experience, providing, 99–105
client focus, 99
client satisfaction with, 4
duties and obligations of, 132
influence on pricing, 115
influences on behavior, 24–25
"lawyers are special" mentality, 37,
110, 152–153
trust in clients, 46, 122
Lean, 64
Lean Six Sigma, 65
learning
client needs, 102, 104
in conscious vs. unconscious mind,
69–70
continuous, 96
loss of, 66–67
from mistakes, 64
sequence of tasks and, 66–67
legal bills review, 122
LegalBizDev, 70
legal business model
billable hour model, 14–15, 43. *See
also* billable hours
changing, vii, xiii, 14–15
legal costs, increases in, 2
legal expenditures. *See also* legal spend
increases in, 2
legal fees
annual growth in, 2–4
realization rates, 3–4
Legal OnRamp, 36
legal profession. *See also* lawyers
changes in, 1, 36
evolution of, 33–36
"more is better" mentality, 8–9, 12, 20
turning point, xi
legal project management, 63–73
key issues, 70–71
*Legal Project Management Quick Reference
Guide* (Hassett), 64n, 70

legal spend
options in reducing, 5
reductions in, 1, 104, 147–154
Lehman Brothers collapse, xi
lessons learned, 93–95, 97
limited resources, allocation of, 57, 61,
75–76, 114
Lippe, Paul, 36
litigation
cost of, 110
process, role of, 70
rules for, 72
spend reduction goals, 104
time of, 110
*Little Rock School Dist. v. Arkansas*, 134
local counsel fees, including in fee
arrangement, 50
lodestar rates, 134–135

## M

managing partners
fee calculation methods, 141–142
pressures on, 25
Model Rule of Professional Conduct 1.5,
127–131
client's ability to pay, 133
commingling money with client
funds, 138
contingency fees, 136
earned fees, 138–139
wasteful and unnecessary procedures,
133
"more is better" mentality, 8–9, 12, 20
"more with less" problem, xii, xiv, 1–2, 4
hourly fees and, 11
solutions, planning, 149, 153
mulligans (do-overs), 119–120
Murphy, James, 94, 96–97

## N

Navy SEALs, 93–95, 159
new clients vs. repeat clients, 108
Novus Law, 68
cost savings from, 152
for document review, 87–91

# O

objectives, setting, 70
operating accounts, unearned funds in, 139
opportunities, influence on pricing, 116–117
opportunities for improvement, identifying, 95
opposing counsel
    influence on pricing, 115
    knowing identity of, 107
organic pricing, 114
orientation of legal profession, 36
Osler, William, 33
outcomes
    costs, reducing, 71. *See also* tools for lowering production costs
    as determination of value, 120–121
    focusing on, xiii, 45–46, 51
    work that influences, 84
outcome success, determining with decision trees, 78, 80
outputs, as client-facing metric, 108
outside counsel
    client relationship management, 100–102
    early case assessment, 59
    evaluation of client position, 57, 61
    and in-house counsel, strain between, 35
    legal spend reductions and, 148
    value of services, 30
outside expenditures, approval process, 49

# P

Parkinson's Law, 115
partners
    fee calculations, 141–142
    mobility of, 5, 8, 148
    pressures on, 25
passive-aggressive behavior, 141
Peer Monitor, 3
*Perdue v. Kenny*, 134–135
performance
    billable hours as measure of, 43
    holdbacks as incentive for, 32, 109
    paying for, 15
    specifying in engagement letter, 48–49
performance-based bonuses, 5
performance-based fees
    reasonableness, 136
    reasonable use of, 137
personal injury cases
    contingency fees in, 136
    decision tree analysis, 78–79
personnel, influence on pricing, 13, 115
Peters, Tom, 63, 100
portfolios of cases, 21
practice of law as business, 37
predictability
    of cost, 7, 15, 27–28, 108, 110
    demand for, 33–34
    with nonhourly billing, 41
    value of, 31–32, 122
pretrial conference checklist, 73–75
previous cases, fees for, 112–113
price-led costing, 149–152
PricewaterhouseCoopers, 68
pricing, 107–122
    checklist for, 179–180
    commercial expectations and, 118
    cost-plus pricing, 150–151
    determining cost, then price, 118
    errors, protection against, 118–122
    factors influencing, 115–117
    fixed monthly fees, 108–109
    historic cluster prices, 113–114
    incremental costs and, 108
    lodestar rates, 134–135
    lowering future prices, 109
    mulligans (do-overs), 119–120
    non-hourly-based rates, 40. *See also* alternative fee arrangements (AFAs); value-based fees
    organic pricing, 114
    past pricing, 112–113
    philosophy of, 108–109
    precepts of, 107–108
    price-led costing, 149–152
    time spent on matters, 114
    time to knowledge, 111–118
    trust and, 122
    value, 121

value-based fees. *See* value-based fees
what-ifs, 121–122
windfalls, 120–121
pricing equations, 40
*Pricing on Purpose: Creating and Capturing Value* (Baker), 149–150
processes
disaggregating, 87–91
engineering, 86–87
error rates, 87
focus on, xiii
task sequencing, 68–70
value-adding and value-preserving, 83
process expenses, reducing, 152
processification, xiii–xiv
process mapping, 63–73
importance of, 71–72
task sequencing, 67–68
production costs. *See* costs of service/production; tools for lowering production costs
productivity
hourly rates and, 7
as results obtained, 42
time and, 42
professional advocates, 123
profitability
cost of service and, 42
generation of, 12–13
and hourly rates, 12
price-led costing and, 149–152
vs. revenue, 9
uncertainty of, 110
profit formula, 53
profit margins
in hourly rates, 110
increasing, 93
of value-based fees, 39
project charters, 159
project management, 63–73
fact accumulation process, 66–67
importance of, 71–72
task sequencing, 67–68

**Q**

quality management, 71
quality metrics for engagements, 42

**R**

rainmakers, 12
realization rates
of blended rates, 19
declines in, 3–4
nonhourly rates and, 41
reasonable fees, 133–135
assessing reasonableness, 128
reasonableness, 128
of contingency and performance-based fees, 137–138
reductions in costs, 6, 114. *See also* tools for lowering production costs
reductions in cycle time, 114
repeat clients vs. new clients, 108
reserves, establishing, 80
resource allocation, 57
appropriate and consistent with client desires, 75–76. *See also* checklists; project management
focused, 114
Restatement (Third) of the Law Governing Lawyers
contingency fees, functions of, 131
contingency fees, reasonableness of, 137
results
fees based on, 46
focus on, xiii, 45–46, 51
outputs, 78, 80
as productivity, 42
retainer agreements, 20–21
advance payment retainer, 124
classic retainer, 123
funds, ownership of, 123–125
recognition of payment as revenue, 47
security retainer, 123–124
and volume discounts, 50–51
revenue
certainty about, 107–108
fixed fees as, 124
focus on, 25
from new vs. repeat clients, 108
vs. profitability, 9
revenue rankings, 8
timing of, 142
reverse contingency fees, 23, 111
review of documents process, 70, 85–91,

144–145
risk
   assessment of, 83–84
   fixed fees and, 109–111
   management of, 83–84
   to schedule or budget, 71
risk sharing, 5, 118
   with contingent and flat fees,
      131–132
   with value-based billing, 15
Roster, Mike, 2
rules, checklists for, 72

# S

savings
   sharing, 23–24, 84
   through disaggregation, 87–91
scheduling risks, assessing, 71
scope of work, 129
   changes, negotiating, 71
   defining, 70
   pricing, 119–120
security retainer agreements, 123–124
Senge, Peter, 97
senior resources, investing in work, 26
service. *See also* costs of service/
      production
   customer service, 30, 100, 105. *See
      also* client experience
   linking with time, 39
settlement
   determining with decision trees, 80
   influence on pricing, 116
   late recommendations for, 57–58
   value of, 77
*7 Habits of Highly Effective People, The*
   (Covey), 149
Seyfarth Lean, 13n10
Seyfarth Shaw, 6, 13
shadow bills, 44–46
shared experiences, learning from, 95
shared savings, 23–24, 84, 87–91
Six Sigma, 64
solutions engineering, 149
spend, legal, 1, 5, 104, 147–154
staffing
   defining roles in engagements, 47–48

influence on pricing, 13, 115
   models of, 103
state court rules on document review, 86
state ethical rules, 136n
status quo, xiii, 1, 7
   vs. change, 156–157
   defense of, 123
STEALTH debriefs, 96–97
Stein, Herbert, 4
stretch goals, 104
success, preparing for, 63–64
Supreme Court *Perdue v. Kenny*,
      134–135
Susskind, Richard, 35–36, 147–148

# T

tasks
   assigning, 71, 85
   identifying, 71
   outside expertise for, 152–153
   practicing into a habit, 68–70
   scheduling, 71
   speed and accuracy, 70
   value-adding and value-preserving, 83
task sequencing
   determining, 67–68
   eliminating waste, 68
teams
   in debriefs, 97
   in direct ECA process, 61
   high-functioning, studying, 159
   influence on pricing, 117
   in-house lawyers on, 105
third-party document review vendors, 87
time. *See also* hourly rates
   influence on pricing, 117
   as measure of value, 45, 120
   productivity and, 42
   and service, linking, 39
   wastes of, 66
timekeeping, costs of, 46
time to knowledge, 111–118
time to trial, influence on pricing, 115
timing of bills and payments, 48
*Tomorrow's Lawyers: An Introduction to
   Your Future* (Susskind), 35, 147n
tools for lowering production costs,

53–55
after-action assessments, 93–98
checklists, 73–76
decision trees, 77–81
disaggregation, 85–91
early case assessment, 57–62
process mapping, 63–73
project management, 63–73
risk management, 83–84
tools of legal profession, 36
trial and trial preparation fees, 50
trust
importance of, 46
in pricing, 119, 122
TyMetrix, 3

**U**

uncertain dollars vs. guaranteed dollars,
107–108
uncertainty, fixed fees and, 109–111
United Technologies, 6
unknowns, addressing, 49–50, 107,
121–122
unnecessary procedures, eliminating, 133
U.S. companies legal costs, 2

**V**

valuation of firm cash capital, 28
value
actions that add and preserve, 83
vs. certainty, 31
outcome as determination of,
120–121
pricing for, 121
provided by legal profession, 36
time as measure of, 45, 120
work value to client, 104–105
Value Adjustment Line (VAL), viii, 105,
121
value-based fees, 8
ABA Model Rules and, 131–132
customer service and, 105
ethical considerations, 128–131
financial rewards with, 16
goals of, 15
profit margins, 39

reasonableness of fees, 128, 133–134
risk conversations, 84
value fee engagement letters, 47–51
Vanguard Software Corporation
DecisionPro software, 80n
virtuous circle, 96
volume discounts, 5, 50–51

**W**

waste elimination, 65, 133
Waterman, Robert H., Jr., 100
what-ifs, 121–122
addressing, 49–50, 107
planning for, 49–50
Whirlpool Corporation, 15
windfalls, 44, 120–121
witness interviews, 59–60
Woldow, Pam, 64n
Wolverine World Wide Inc., 147
work
to be performed, specifying, 48–49
forecasts of, 46
influence on pricing, 116
tracking, 44
wasted time, removing, 66–67
work plan approach, 44
work product quality, 145
World Health Organization's Safe
Surgery Saves Lives program, 72
written agreements on fee arrangements,
139

## The Lawyer's Guide to Microsoft® Outlook 2013
### By Ben M. Schorr
Product Code: 5110752 • **LP Price:** $41.95 • **Regular Price:** $69.95

Take control of your e-mail, calendar, to-do list, and more with The Lawyer's Guide to Microsoft® Outlook 2013. This essential guide summarizes the most important new features in the newest version of Microsoft® Outlook and provides practical tips that will promote organization and productivity in your law practice. Written specifically for lawyers by a twenty-year veteran of law office technology and ABA member, this book is a must-have.

## Internet Legal Research on a Budget
### By Carole A. Levitt and Judy Davis
Product Code: 5110778 • **LP Price:** $69.95 • **Regular Price:** $89.95

With cost-conscious clients scrutinizing legal bills, lawyers cannot afford to depend on expensive legal research databases, especially when reliable free resources are available. Internet Legal Research on a Budget: Free and Low-Cost Resources for Lawyers will help you quickly find the best free or low-cost resources online and use them for your research needs. The authors share the top websites, apps, blogs, Twitter feeds, and crowdsourced resources that will save you time, money, and frustration during the legal research progress.

## The 2014 Solo and Small Firm Legal Technology Guide
### By Sharon D. Nelson, John W. Simek, Michael C. Maschke
Product Code: 5110774 • **LP Price:** $54.95 • **Regular Price:** $89.95

This annual guide is the only one of its kind written to help solo and small firm lawyers find the best technology for their dollar. You'll find the most current information and recommendations on computers, servers, networking equipment, legal software, printers, security products, smartphones, the iPad, and anything else a law office might need. It's written in clear, easily understandable language to make implementation easier if you choose to do it yourself, or you can use it in conjunction with your IT consultant. Either way, you'll learn how to make technology work for you.

## Entertainment Careers for Lawyers, 3rd Ed.
### By William D. Henslee
Product Code: 5110769 • **LP Price:** $32.95 • **Regular Price:** $54.95

*Entertainment Careers for Lawyers, Third Edition*, will dispel many of the myths surrounding the practice and help lawyers and law students gain an understanding of the realities of entertainment law. Written by William D. Henslee, an experienced entertainment lawyer and law professor, this book will help you gain an overview of the substantive law areas included in entertainment law, from intellectual property and litigation to contract negotiations and estate planning. You will also earn about the career trajectories available in four major entertainment genres: music, theater, film, and television.

## LinkedIn in One Hour for Lawyers, 2nd Ed.
### By Dennis Kennedy and Allison C. Shields
Product Code: 5110773 • **LP Price:** $39.95 • **Regular Price:** $49.95

Since the first edition of LinkedIn in One Hour for Lawyers was published, LinkedIn has added almost 100 million users, and more and more lawyers are using the platform on a regular basis. Now, this bestselling ABA book has been fully revised and updated to reflect significant changes to LinkedIn's layout and functionality made through 2013.

## Alternative Fees for Business Lawyers and Their Clients
### By Mark A. Robertson
Product Code: 5110781 • **LP Price:** $59.95 • **Regular Price:** $79.95

The use of alternative fee arrangements by lawyers and the demand for those arrangements by clients is increasing. How are you and your law firm addressing this threat to the billable hour? Are you prepared to recognize that value is not measured in one-tenth-of-an-hour increments? Alternative Fees for Business Lawyers and Their Clients addresses how large firm, small firm, and solo lawyers can implement and evaluate alternative fee arrangements in transactional matters. This essential guide also provides real case studies of business lawyers and firms successfully using alternative fee arrangements to deliver value to both the clients and the lawyers.

## Succeeding as Outside Counsel
### By Rod Boddie
Product Code: 5110766 • **LP Price:** $59.95 • **Regular Price:** $79.95

The delivery of quality legal services requires that lawyers function as customer service representatives as well as legal technicians. *Succeeding as Outside Counsel* was written by an in-house lawyer with over 15 years of experience managing and utilizing the services of outside counsel. As a result, this book provides outside counsel with practical guidance on how to improve the level of service they provide and how to deepen their relationships with their clients—all from a client's perspective. This essential guide will discuss how outside counsel have excelled, where they have fallen short, and what they need to do to serve the comprehensive needs of the client by adding value that goes far beyond any individual matter.

## Personal Branding in One Hour for Lawyers
### By Katy Goshtasbi
Product Code: 5110765 • **LP Price:** $39.95 • **Regular Price:** $49.95

With over 1.2 million licensed attorneys in the United States, how do lawyers stand out from their fellow practitioners and get jobs, promotions, clients, and referrals? To survive and thrive, lawyers must develop their own intentional personal brand to distinguish themselves from the competition. Personal branding expert and experienced attorney Katy Goshtasbi explains how attorneys can highlight their unique talents and abilities, manage their perceptions, and achieve greater success as a lawyer in the process.

## The Lawyer's Guide to Microsoft® Word 2013
**By Ben M. Schorr**

Product Code: 5110757 • LP Price: $41.95 • Regular Price: $69.95

Microsoft® Word is one of the most used applications in the Microsoft® Office suite. This handy reference includes clear explanations, legal-specific descriptions, and time-saving tips for getting the most out of Microsoft Word®--and customizing it for the needs of today's legal professional. Focusing on the tools and features that are essential for lawyers in their everyday practice, *The Lawyer's Guide to Microsoft® Word 2013* explains in detail the key components to help make you more effective, more efficient, and more successful. Written specifically for lawyers by a twenty-year veteran of legal technology, this guide will introduce you to Microsoft® Word 2013.

## Legal Project Management in One Hour for Lawyers
**By Pamela H. Woldow and Douglas B. Richardson**

Product Code: 5110763 • LP Price: $39.95 • Regular Price: $49.95

Legal clients are responding to today's unprecedented financial pressures by demanding better predictability, cost-effectiveness and communication from their outside legal service providers. They give their business to those who can manage legal work efficiently--and take it away from those who can't or won't. *Legal Project Management in One Hour for Lawyers* provides any attorney with practical skills and methods for improving efficiency, keeping budgets under control, building strong working relationships with clients, and maximizing profitability.

## Adobe Acrobat in One Hour for Lawyers
**By Ernie Svenson**

Product Code: 5110768 • LP Price: $39.95 • Regular Price: $49.95

Most lawyers now encounter PDFs, and many own Adobe Acrobat--the most widely used software for working with PDFs. But most attorneys are confused about how to work efficiently with PDFs. *Adobe Acrobat in One Hour for Lawyers* is written for lawyers and legal professionals who want to be more organized by making better use of PDFs.

## Quickbooks in One Hour for Lawyers
**By Lynette Benton**

Product Code: 5110764 • LP Price: $39.95 • Regular Price: $49.95

Spend more time practicing law--and less time balancing the books--by investing in easy and effective accounting software. Lynette Benton, a QuickBooks certified ProAdvisor and consultant who has helped hundreds of attorneys and small firms with financial management, will teach you to use this popular accounting software in your law practice. *QuickBooks in One Hour for Lawyers* offers step-by-step guidance for getting started with QuickBooks and putting it to work tracking income, expenses, time, billing, and much more.

## WordPress in One Hour for Lawyers: How to Create a Website for Your Law Firm
**By Jennifer Ellis**

Product Code: 5110767 • LP Price: $39.95 • Regular Price: $49.95

Law firms without websites are placing themselves at a great disadvantage compared with the competition. Even if you feel you receive the majority of your clients through referrals, a website provides the opportunity for those potential clients to learn about you and your firm. This book will explain how to get create your firm's website quickly and easily with WordPress®software.

## Twitter in One Hour for Lawyers
**By Jared Correia**

Product Code: 5110746 • LP Price: $24.95 • Regular Price: $39.95

More lawyers than ever before are using Twitter to network with colleagues, attract clients, market their law firms, and even read the news. But to the uninitiated, Twitter's short messages, or tweets, can seem like they are written in a foreign language. Twitter in One Hour for Lawyers will demystify one of the most important social-media platforms of our time and teach you to tweet like an expert.

## Virtual Law Practice: How to Deliver Legal Services Online
**By Stephanie L. Kimbro**

Product Code: 5110707 • LP Price: $47.95 • Regular Price: $79.95

The legal market has recently experienced a dramatic shift as lawyers seek out alternative methods of practicing law and providing more affordable legal services. Virtual law practice is revolutionizing the way the public receives legal services and how legal professionals work with clients.

## Worldox in One Hour for Lawyers
**By John Heckman**

Product Code: 5110771 • LP Price: $39.95 • Regular Price: $49.95

Never lose another document or waste valuable time searching for one. In just one hour, learn how to organize your documents and e-mails electronically with Worldox software. Veteran law-firm technology consult John Heckman reveals what Worldox will do for your firm--and how to customize its features for the specific needs of your practice.

## PowerPoint in One Hour for Lawyers
**By Paul J. Unger**

Product Code: 5110705 • LP Price: $39.95 • Regular Price: $49.95

The difference between a successful presentation and an unsuccessful one can often be traced to a presenter's use--or misuse--of PowerPoint®. *PowerPoint in One Hour for Lawyers* offers practical advice for creating effective presentations quickly and easily. PowerPoint expert and attorney Paul Unger will help you avoid mishaps and develop a compelling presentation using storyboarding techniques.

# 30-DAY RISK-FREE ORDER FORM

**ABALAW
PRACTICE
DIVISION**
The Business of Practicing Law

Please print or type. To ship UPS, we must have your street address.
If you list a P.O. Box, we will ship by U.S. Mail.

Name

Member ID

Firm/Organization

Street Address

City/State/Zip

Area Code/Phone (In case we have a question about your order)

E-mail

**Method of Payment:**
☐ Check enclosed, payable to American Bar Association
☐ MasterCard       ☐ Visa       ☐ American Express

Card Number                    Expiration Date

Signature Required

**MAIL THIS FORM TO:**
**American Bar Association**, Publication Orders
P.O. Box 10892, Chicago, IL 60610

**ORDER BY PHONE:**
24 hours a day, 7 days a week:
Call 1-800-285-2221 to place a credit card
order. We accept Visa, MasterCard, and
American Express.

**EMAIL ORDERS:** orders@americanbar.org
**FAX ORDERS:** 1-312-988-5568

**VISIT OUR WEB SITE: www.ShopABA.org**
Allow 7-10 days for regular UPS delivery. Need it
sooner? Ask about our overnight delivery options.
Call the ABA Service Center at 1-800-285-2221
for more information.

**GUARANTEE:**
If—for any reason—you are not satisfied with your
purchase, you may return it within 30 days of
receipt for a refund of the price of the book(s).
No questions asked.

***Thank You For Your Order.***

Join the ABA Law Practice Division today and receive a substantial discount on Division publications!

| Product Code: | Description: | Quantity: | Price: | Total Price: |
|---|---|---|---|---|
| | | | | $ |
| | | | | $ |
| | | | | $ |
| | | | | $ |
| | | | | $ |

| **\*\*Shipping/Handling:** | | **\*Tax:** | | |
|---|---|---|---|---|
| $0.00 to $9.99 | add $0.00 | IL residents add 9.25% | **Subtotal:** | $ |
| $10.00 to $49.99 | add $6.95 | DC residents add 5.75% | **\*Tax:** | $ |
| $50.00 to $99.99 | add $8.95 | | **\*\*Shipping/Handling:** | $ |
| $100.00 to $199.99 | add $10.95 | Yes, I am an ABA member and would like to join the Law Practice Division today! (Add $50.00) | | $ |
| $200.00 to $499.99 | add $13.95 | | **Total:** | $ |